THE ULTIMATE BOOK OF
SMALL GARDENS

THE ULTIMATE BOOK OF
SMALL GARDENS

Graham Rice

Photography by judywhite

CASSELL
ILLUSTRATED

First published in Great Britain in 2004 by Cassell Illustrated,
a division of Octopus Publishing Group Limited
2–4 Heron Quays, London E14 4JP

Distributed in the United States of America by
Sterling Publishing Co., Inc.,
387 Park Avenue South, New York, NY 10016-8810

A CIP catalogue record for this book is available from the British Library.

ISBN 1 84403 150 0

Printed in China

For my Mum and Dad, Doris and Freddie Rice, whose own small garden has been a constant joy in their long and happy life together.

Contents

Introduction

What is a Small Garden?

'Let me caution all, not to undertake more than can be well looked after with hands enough for the well management of things in their proper season; for a small Plot of ground well ordered, turns to greater advantage than a large one neglected...'

Leonard Meager, *The New Art of Gardening*, 1697

In 1952 Brigadier C. E. Lucas Phillips first published *The Small Garden*, a classic, and an invaluable book whose sound and cheerful advice helped many new gardeners learn about gardening without it seeming a chore. In it he tells us what he means by a small garden: 'I have borne in mind a limit of about an acre...' (about half a hectare).

Gardens have changed a great deal since then, and an acre would now be thought of as a huge garden. His assumption that people with a garden half that size would have the help of a gardener also adds an additional air of unreality. So in this book, I make no such assumptions about size. Instead, I have opted for practical realism and taken to heart the words of Leonard Meager (above).

I will not be rigid and insist that a small garden must be, for example, less than a quarter of an acre, or 1,000 square yards, or 250 square metres/300 square yards. Apart from anything else, few novice gardeners can visualize a garden of 1,000 square yards. I prefer to use measures that relate to the gardener rather than to the garden.

First of all there's time. A garden 10m/30ft square may be too large if the gardener works night shifts, travels all over the world or simply dislikes gardening. Perhaps, like Leonard Meager, I could suggest that a small garden is one that can be managed comfortably by the gardener concerned – and for some people a balcony will be too large. But I would expect a small garden to require at most no more than an hour or two's care at the weekend

plus the occasional summer evening. I do not expect paid help to be available.

Second, you can measure a garden according to the inclination and enthusiasm of the gardener. Any garden that frustrates the gardener by its restricted size could be described as small – or perhaps that should be phrased more carefully: a garden is small if the gardener must constantly consider how all the plants, features and activities he or she wishes to accommodate can actually be fitted in.

This book will help you fit in more of everything than you ever thought possible without overcrowding, and explain how to create it and maintain it all effectively without lavish expenditure. Crucial to the enjoyment of

a small garden is the realization that three things combine to make it satisfying: appropriate design, thoughtful planning and not being overburdened with the garden's care. In some ways we may treat our garden like an outdoor room, but it's the plants that will make it special. So the choice of plants is designed to provide colour, interest and food all the year round. And that is possible in even the smallest of gardens.

Graham Rice

Chapter 1

Making the Most of a Small Space

The one thing that the size of a garden should never restrict is the imagination. True, there will be no room for fishing lakes, tennis courts or avenues of stately oaks in a small garden, and it would be a mistake to attempt to replicate such schemes in miniature. But in the same way as there is a challenge in planting a park effectively, there is as much of a challenge in deciding how to plant that room outside your back door.

Your small garden

At its best a small garden functions as an extra, outdoor room. There may be cupboards (shed) and cooking facilities (barbecue) but there will also be the 'floor' (lawn or paving) and décor (plants). The crucial difference between an indoor and an outdoor room is not, strangely, their location. The crucial factor is change: a garden is constantly changing because it is furnished with living organisms that respond to the seasons, and it's this change that gives a garden its special appeal. A small garden should be planted to reflect the constantly changing year, and planned so that it's possible to enjoy as much of this seasonal change as possible.

Practicalities

We have to live in this outdoor room, however, and in a small space where there's little leeway for error, the functional elements must work efficiently. Access to storage, to activity areas of various sorts and for maintenance should give us as little concern as a good carpet inside the house – and need rather less regular attention. You would never put the drinks cabinet or the kitchen equipment you use most in the least accessible place, so don't keep the rubbish bin where it's furthest from the back door and from access to the street.

Personal taste

When it comes to décor, you don't put up with the horrid wallpaper left by your predecessor or forget to match your new scheme to the style of the house and its situation. With plants as with paints, wall-coverings, ornaments and works of art, there's a vast, ever-increasing and sometimes bewildering choice available. Never assume that you can get it right first time without a little guidance – either from this book or from friends, magazines, the internet and television.

Plants, of course, provide the opportunities for personalization, and if chosen carefully, they can enhance those changes that the seasons inexorably bring. One plant can provide four or five visual changes over the course of a year, and just one square yard of garden can be constantly captivating – beats lawn any day.

Don't be afraid to stick to what you feel is right even if it's unconventional. A garden should be furnished and decorated in a way that reflects your character just as your living-room does. It won't be possible to do everything all at once, especially as plants take time to mature, but contentment in the room outside is an achievable goal.

You and your needs

The features and plantings that form a garden, and the activities that take place in it, vary enormously. You have your own special priorities and preferences, which blend to create a unique combination - your own garden. You may have one special idea that dominates your thinking, or there may be competing demands including those from other members of the family. Establishing priorities and integrating them to form a cohesive whole can be difficult, so it seems wise to start by discussing the possibilities.

Atmosphere

Creating an atmosphere in which you feel comfortable comes naturally to some and is bewildering to others. In a garden, atmosphere depends on developing a structure in sympathy with the house and with your own tastes, adding features that are within your budget and within your capacity to build well, choosing colours, tones and styles that tune with your own emotional inclinations, then planting in a way that is cohesive and provides colour, interest, subtlety and perhaps food when you want it – preferably all the year round.

OPPOSITE: Surround seats with aromatic permanent plantings and use pots to provide a series of changing seasonal flowers.

A crucial part of achieving these objectives is to be ruthless. It's important to tolerate nothing that spoils the effect you have in mind, for in a small garden eyesores like a tumbledown fence, a cracked and crumbling path or a dying tree have so much more impact than they would in a broader space where they're not constantly in your gaze; in a small garden they constantly offend.

So my top priority is to do something – don't just sit back and dither. You wouldn't do that with a new living room; don't do it in your new garden either.

Entertaining

Entertaining outside demands both a congenial environment and appropriate facilities. If the garden gives you, your family and your guests an uneasy feeling, no one will enjoy your parties. As well as fostering a welcoming atmosphere, you'll need a firm, level area for seats and for standing and somewhere for the barbecue. This can either be built into a wall or be portable and freestanding, in which case you'll need somewhere to store it. You don't necessarily need a lawn.

Your entertaining area (let's call it the patio) can consist of a small paved area near the house or can take up most of a town garden, with the planting around it. Don't feel that you have to be conventional; if you think that most of your enclosed garden should be paved, then go ahead and pave it.

Food

If you want to grow food crops, you can usually find the space even in a small garden. A growing bag will hold three tomato plants; runner beans, gooseberries or a peach can be trained on the fence, a grapevine around the door; you can mark out a small plot for summer crops, or perhaps a larger one for cordon apples or cut-and-come-again salads. Whether on a small scale or as a top priority, food plants can always find a productive home. And there's always room for herbs – in the garden, in pots or on the windowsill.

Play

Kids need somewhere outside to play, and in a small garden other plans may need to be delayed until the wear and tear the children create is less of a factor. A lawn may be an important requirement, or perhaps a soft-surface play area; the likelihood of ball games may suggest waiting before building a conservatory

LEFT: Bright colours and strong shapes help make this playpit appealing to kids. It can be repainted and turned into a planter when they grow up.

OPPOSITE: Not insisting on a lawn opens up opportunities for bringing water and planting close to the house.

or greenhouse. It may be wise not to use gravel and so avoid too many scrapes. In general, it pays to wait before creating carefully planned plantings and fragile features until the children are older and their activities will not cause so much damage.

Plants

Some gardeners fill their plots with plants, retaining only a small area for sitting and a winding path through the vegetation. Others are less single-minded, but if plants are not seen as fundamental, you might as well build an extension to the house. The infinite variety of easy-to-grow plants that are widely available, and the many ways they can be used, give gardens their unique character and allow a continual refreshing state of change, from day to day, week to week, season to season and year to year.

Plants dominate most gardens; not in the sense of spreading, towering over you and erupting through the paving, but because their character and the way in which they're used will be fundamental in creating the atmosphere, providing the colour and interest, setting the style and providing year-round pleasure.

Practical and functional

Many families have uses for the garden that do not involve plants or entertaining: hanging out washing, repairing motorbikes, golf practice, archery, sculpting, stripping paint off old doors; the atmosphere and the plants may be strictly secondary. If this is the case, all you need is a large, well-drained paved area and perhaps a lean-to glass roof – like a conservatory with no sides. And you need good access, an accessible drain, an outside tap and an outside power point. This is the only place in the book where such activities will be considered. This is, after all, a book for gardeners, not dirt bike riders.

Working from home

For those who work from home, the garden can also provide a setting that certainly beats the back bedroom or fourteenth floor of a tower block. A table and chair,

an umbrella to provide necessary shade for the laptop screen, perhaps even a power point and phone point in a waterproof cabinet inset into a wall where books and stationery can also be temporarily stored. Just think: when you get a business call on your mobile and are asked where you are you can say: 'I'm at the office' – and be smelling the roses.

Relaxing

Simple relaxation is perhaps the garden's most important use. It should be a haven from the bustle at work, in the kitchen and on the school run, a place to recuperate, meditate and recharge. You need a patio with a table and chairs, a sun lounger or hammock, a bench – or just four slabs on which to stand a chair. You'll soon realize that even in a small town garden you'll need more than one sitting area. The sun moves round, and you'll want to move into its warmth or out of its heat. Some areas must be accessible in slippers or bare feet, some must be screened from neighbours. For you to make the most of your garden it must be private, comfortable, quiet and easy to flop into at all times.

Time available

If you have a busy job, or if both you and your partner have demanding careers (and/or a demanding family), there's no point in planning a complicated design full of features and plantings that require regular and detailed attention; unless you're going to pay someone to look after it all for you, it's just not going to happen.

Primary uses of the garden

Outdoor room, playing field, mechanic's workshop, botanic garden, dog's toilet – people have different requirements from their garden. If you like to use your garden as a summer room outside, it must have a broad open space, some hard surfaces and be light and

sheltered. If the whole family is out all day, a west-facing sitting area for relaxing after work is imperative. If football practice is top priority, you need a broad sweep of well-drained lawn surrounded by high fences. If it's plants that matter, you will need to create different conditions for different plants and you may want little more than a meandering path through a garden packed with flowers and foliage. As for the dog... dogs can be trained to use one small area of a garden so the rest of the garden is not fouled – but it takes determination. The cat, of course, will have a mind of its own.

Financial considerations

Your plans must, of course, match your budget. At the top end of the scale, you can organize a loan to have your garden designed, built and planted – lenders recognize that a beautiful garden adds value to your property. (This may be practical when interest rates are low, but not when they're high.)

Professional design is expensive, but can be excellent value for money if you have specific requirements and

apparently insoluble problems. Hard landscape (paving, gravel, walls, fences and the like) costs a lot more than soft landscape (lawns and plants). But don't be deceived. A garden with lawns and plants raised from seed or given by friends and family can look as good and be as enjoyable as one designed and made by professionals with the finest stone and the choicest plants.

Personal enthusiasms

If you like to keep koi carp, investigate the best situation for their pond before doing any work on the garden. If you want to play badminton, allow a generous area for play or the flowerbeds will be trampled. If you'd like to grow a collection of special plants – woodland plants or alpines, for example – consider their requirements and don't put the shed in the spot that suits them best.

The garden-to-be

Before you can think about creating the garden you want, you need to take a good look at what you already have. Even the garden of a new building will have features that you must take into account, whether they're just a manhole cover and some rubble or fences and a path.

What have you got?

Gazing optimistically from the kitchen window on a sunny Sunday morning is not the best way to assess the garden of your brand new home. You should go out, in your boots if necessary, and take a closer look. Where does the sun rise, more or less? OK, now work out where south is; that will tell you which are the sunniest and the shadiest parts of the garden and where you need to sit to relax in the evening sun after work. This is important information.

Builders' rubbish and spillage

Are there any obvious piles of builders' rubbish? This can vary from bags of rock-solid cement to hardcore, scrap metal and timber, piles of sawdust, teapots and

beer cans, old newspapers, sheets of plastic and worse. If there's more than will go into two or three stout fertilizer sacks – and if there's some on view there's bound to be more buried underneath – collect it and get rid of it all as soon as possible. Don't use flimsy kitchen bin bags – they will burst.

Investigate what's underground. If there's any wire or metal peeping from the soil waiting to trip you up, look closer. The worst offenders are discarded reinforcing rods that go under the fence and end up under next door's path. Dig them out as best you can, and cooperate with your neighbour if necessary. Occasionally you'll find that these steel rods end in a large block of concrete. Use a club hammer and steel bolster to break it up without moving it; the pieces can then be removed relatively easily.

Old chain-link fencing is an especially infuriating problem, as it may be dumped, flat, under the soil, perhaps over a wide area. Even if you intend laying

ABOVE: A neglected garden provides the perfect blank canvas. Assess soil, light levels and aspect before deciding how to develop the space.

OPPOSITE: It's important to prioritize in a small space. Here a hot tub and pond, camouflaged with plants in containers, provide a functional alternative to a lawn or traditional beds and borders.

a lawn, remove it, as you'll only find it again in a year or two when you come to dig a pond or plant a tree. Find and expose one edge first, then proceed across the netting, moving the soil behind you and rolling the netting as you go.

Soil type

Having removed the rubbish, you're now in a position to examine the soil. There are two sad (horticultural) consequences of shoddy building work. First, the nasty, infertile subsoil could now be on the top and all the rich topsoil buried (or even removed altogether and sold to someone else). Second, machinery may have compacted the soil so much that it's difficult even to force a spade in without cursing. Water may also drain away very slowly.

The first way to assess your soil is simply by looking at it. If it's black, that's a very good sign. If it's very dark brown, that's quite good too. If it's yellow, pale brown, grey, streaky or mottled, that's less good. The blacker it

is, the more organic matter it contains; the more organic matter there is, the easier the soil will be to work, the better your plants will grow and the less you'll have to water them. Now pick some soil up and rub it between your fingers. If it feels smooth and a bit like kids' play clay, and sticks together in a lump, that means it has a lot of clay in it. If you can see the stones, it's (you've guessed) stony, and if it falls apart quickly and feels slightly gritty, it's sandy.

Soil that is predominantly clay, often turned up from below during building, poses the most problems but can end up being the most fertile.

Clay soils:
- are sticky;
- are badly drained;
- are difficult to dig or hoe when wet;
- stick together in big clods;
- stick to your shoes when wet;
- crack badly when dry;
- hold water well;
- hold plant foods well;
- are potentially very fertile.

There are two ways of improving clay soil: you can add garden compost or organic matter such as soil improver from the garden centre, or you can add gritty material such as sharp sand or fine gravel. Organic matter increases fertility and helps improve drainage; grit only improves drainage. The branded preparations advertised for curing the problems of clay soils are expensive. Your money is better spent on a few bags of soil improver.

Soil that is sandy or gravelly is easier to dig and hoe but needs more water and more feeding.

Sandy soils:
- are well drained;
- are easy to work, even shortly after rain;
- need plenty of watering;
- let plant foods wash out quickly and therefore need more feeding.

Here again organic matter is the answer, as it holds water and plant foods in the soil without making the soil sticky.

It's simple really: whatever your soil, adding organic matter is usually the answer.

Acid or limy?

The acidity, or otherwise, of the soil is measured on the pH scale. The pH level of soil matters because it governs which plants you can grow easily. Most soils are in the range of about 5.5. to 7.5, with 6.5 a rough average (7.0 is neutral). If a soil is too limy (well above 7.0), or too acid (well below 7.0), soil nutrients may be less available to particular plants.

At the garden centre you can buy a simple and inexpensive pH test kit to tell you roughly how limy or acid your soil is; get one because knowing the acidity or alkalinity of your soil will help you to choose plants that will flourish in your garden. Acid soils will grow good rhododendrons, azaleas, heathers and lupins, and tend to produce blue hydrangeas; alkaline soils will grow good broccoli, cabbages, viburnums and wild meadow flowers, and tend to produce pink hydrangeas.

Walls

If your garden is a new one, your only walls are likely to be the house walls, although you may be lucky enough to have one or more boundary walls as well. There's nothing more useful around a garden than a 1.8m/6ft wall, as it provides privacy, shelter, useful shade and a warm 'storage heater' for sun-loving and tender plants.

Never be afraid to plant self-clinging climbers up new walls; the wall will not be damaged. Never plant them on old walls with soft mortar; their roots will loosen the old soft mortar, which will then drop out and expose the wall to the weather. Allow for planting areas at the base of walls when planning paving. Lower walls are sometimes provided as boundaries, and these are usually best enhanced by fixing trellis on top to bring them up to about 1.8m/6ft. The trellis also provides a ready-made support for plants.

ABOVE: If you move into a new house and find azaleas like these in your garden, or the gardens of your neighbours, then your soil is acid.

OPPOSITE: Ornamental kales, here with budding chrysanthemums, thrive best in alkaline soils, as do their edible relations.

BELOW: If your soil holds together in a sticky ball when you squeeze it, you can be sure that it contains a high proportion of clay and will not drain well.

Fences

Your new garden is much more likely to be provided with fences than with walls. These can range from two or three sagging strands of wire, through chain-link wire fences, to square-pattern wooden trellis – the more elegant trellis patterns are rarely used on new developments. Lapboard timber fencing is more solid, and feathered board fencing is the most solid timber fencing of all (see page 51).

Regard loose strands of wire as temporary; they won't even keep the dog in – or out. Chain-link fencing at least keeps most dogs from roaming (in or out) and provides a good support for annual climbers. Trellis is excellent, as it provides an effective barrier, a good support for climbing plants and lessens the sense of enclosure, creating a relaxed atmosphere in a small space.

Builders often provide lapboard or woven fencing for small gardens and, as they weather, these make a good background for plants, allowing you to forget the boundaries for a few years. Woven fencing is less sturdy and less soundproof than lapboard, and is often warped, though still standing, after five years. The really heavy-duty, close-boarded style is rarely used except where the fence backs on to a busy path or roadway. You should be well pleased with it.

No boundaries

On some developments neither the front nor the back gardens will be fenced. If all you feel you need at the back is a prospect of green lawn, leave it at that and simply buy a mower (or hire a contractor). Otherwise, try to install all the fencing at the same time. If you have a contractor do the job, it will work out cheaper; if you do it yourself, having the job half finished will nag at you when you should be relaxing.

Manhole covers

Some architects have no idea about manholes. They site them where most sane people would put the patio, and

OPPOSITE: Traditional planting often looks surprisingly effective when set against the clean lines of a more contemporary paving design.

you then have to cope with an infuriating obstacle. In fact you can deal with a manhole, wherever it is, as long as you note its surface level and appreciate that this dictates the level of the surrounding paving or soil. You must not bury it or you may not be able to unblock your drains in an emergency.

Manhole covers can be disguised. You can buy recessed planting covers that provide space to fill with compost before planting, and there are also recessed covers designed to be filled with the same paving material that surrounds the manhole. Spreading plants can be set alongside. The manhole can even be raised or lowered (by a builder, please) to a more convenient level. But remember, one day you may need to remove the lid – and quickly.

Concrete house surrounds

New houses, especially bungalows, are often blessed with a concrete surround about 60cm/2ft wide that runs like a path all the way round the foot of the house wall. This pointless and unattractive border effectively stops you from planting any climbers on the wall and also neatly prevents the house from ever melding into the garden. You can stand pots there, I suppose, but sooner or later, if you're serious about plants, the concrete will have to go. Hire a pneumatic hammer – better still, hire the operator as well. The hardcore your demolition produces can be used as the base for new paths.

Paths and drives

Your new garden may not even have a path to the front door, but at least this enables you to lay your own exactly where you want it. Don't plan anything too fancy or indirect. You may be provided with a straight path up to the door, which is fine. The path may be combined with the drive to the garage, and there's not much you can do about that without further recourse to the pneumatic hammer. Don't forget that you can move the entrance to your property to a new position in the road, although you may need permission from the local authority.

Influences outside the garden

Now that much more attention is being paid to retaining mature trees on new housing developments, you may find one or more of them growing in or overhanging your new and empty garden. It may shade your windows, its leaves (or worse, its roots) may clog up your drains and its piddly little pears may litter your new lawn.

If the tree is growing next door, you're entitled to remove any branches that project over your side of the boundary. But if you must let in a little more light, cooperate with your new neighbour and agree for a branch to be removed at the trunk. Do it sensitively. In practice, machinery may remove the lower branches, intentionally or otherwise, during building. Any tree subject to a Tree Preservation Order must not be pruned, let alone removed, without permission. Note where the tree is in relation to the sun and where its shadow falls. The soil will be drier under its branches,

and even a tall, upright conifer with no branches overhanging your side will have roots taking moisture and plant nutrients from your soil.

Looking at neighbours' gardens

You can get some idea of how your garden will develop by looking at those of your neighbours and seeing what flourishes in them. If their gardens are full of weeds, yours may be too. Not because the local soil is inherently full of weed roots and seeds, but because seed from nearby will blow into your plot. If your neighbours grow verdant nettles, the soil is probably fertile. And if they grow good rhododendrons or blue hydrangeas, you will know at once that the soil is acid – you too will be able to grow them, together with azaleas, pieris and other woodland plants. If there

ABOVE: A single plant of an aromatic herb like this French lavender can create an atmospheric aroma alongside a patio in a small space.

are clovers and buddleias, then rhododendrons and azaleas are unlikely to thrive.

Initial planning

Ensuring that you site the basic, immovable features in the right place will make life so much easier later that it's worth putting a little thought into it right at the start.

Bins

How far do you want to walk with your rubbish? How far do you want to cart the bin for the binmen to pick up? Not far, in either case. Site your bin near the back door and near the exit to the street. It's best to put it in a corner, where plants can be set around it or an elegant piece of timber fencing or even walling can screen it unobtrusively. But don't just put up a small piece of screening that doesn't merge with the rest of the garden – you might as well look at the bin.

Clothesline

Gone are the days of the long straight path alongside the long straight clothesline. I'm sure it only encouraged long straight borders with long straight edges. Then everyone dozed off. And growing a grapevine up the clothes pole was never a very good idea. The washing whirly that fits into a hole in the patio is only there when you need it, all the washing is just a short walk from the house so you can get there quickly when it rains, and you can go out in your slippers if you feel like it. Build a little hideaway near the bins to store the beast when it's party time. Better still, buy a tumble dryer.

Patio

Whichever direction the back of your house faces, you need a sitting area there – you won't always want to walk to the far corner of the garden for a brief rest. The most important place for a patio, however, is facing west or south-west, so that for as much of the year as possible you can sit in the sun when you get home from work. And on those warm summer evenings, your alfresco parties will catch the very last of the sun.

Of course, in a very small garden where there's no grass and all the unplanted area is paved, you can sit anywhere that takes your fancy, in sun or shade.

Paths

The garden with no grass will be all path in the same way as it is all patio, and this is the best solution for the smallest areas. Paths in all-paved areas can also be created by mixing materials, such as a path of tiles within a paving of brick. If you intend to make paths through or around lawns, don't plan them as stepping stones in the grass; not only do you have to set the height just right to avoid snagging the mower or stepping into a hole, but you have to clip the grass round each one. Life's too short.

A diagonal path will make the garden look bigger, as will one that narrows a little as it goes away from the house. A slightly curved path, or one of irregular width with dwarf, overhanging plants, looks better than a straight one with bare parallel sides.

Shed

In a small garden you cannot avoid seeing your shed, so there's no point in trying to hide it – though it can be camouflaged with climbers, of course. The first question is: what are you going to keep in it? If the answer is bicycles – put it near the gate or the access to the street; garden tools – anywhere; workbench – anywhere; pram – near the street access and the house; armchair and bottle of Scotch – as far away from the commotion of the house as possible; artist's easel and watercolours – allow for a long window on the north side.

Looking at the problem from another angle: which is the worst patch of soil or the place most unsuited to plants? Put the shed there.

Conservatory

It's surprising how many people put the conservatory or sunroom in a place where they have to go out of the house to get into it. Ensure that you can walk straight in, through patio or French doors if possible, so that it really is an extra room. Also, try to site it against a wall

with a radiator on the inside – that way you can heat the conservatory by adding an extra radiator without too much new pipework. Don't forget power points and a water tap.

If your conservatory is north-facing, it will need constant heating to keep it warm in winter, and this may create a dry atmosphere unsuitable for many plants. If it's east-facing, it will warm up well in the morning, and the sacrifice of an outdoor east wall is not significant – east walls are not good spots for many plants. South-facing conservatories will become very, very hot in summer and need generous ventilation and blinds to keep them comfortable; they'll be cosy and warm on sunny winter days. Those that are west-facing are warm on autumn evenings, prolonging the summer as long as possible.

Barbecue

If you plan to use your garden for entertaining during the summer months, it makes sense to build a barbecue outside while building your patio and surrounding walling. It can be built of similar materials and can even have coordinated seating and storage, so harmonizing with its surroundings. A freestanding mobile barbecue can be left outside all winter but will last longer and work better if stored in the dry; consider where.

Compost heap

A compost heap is useful in even the smallest garden. Neither manufactured plastic bins nor home-made timber ones are especially elegant, so are best sited in a discreet corner. But remember that they need moisture, either from rain or from a hosepipe.

Power

Electricity, for a pool pump, for outdoor lighting and for a waterproof outdoor power point for a mower

and other equipment, is best considered right at the start so that the main cables can go under paths where there's no chance of disturbance. Get a qualified electrician to do the job for you to ensure maximum safety, and never forget the circuit breaker.

Water

In a very small garden, one outside tap should be sufficient to meet your needs; don't forget to install a tap in the conservatory as well. Run the conservatory water pipes underneath the flooring to come up in a corner.

How to plan

Planning a garden is always necessary, and a few weeks or months of thought and family discussion are worth any amount of rushing in foolishly only to repent and decide you need to change everything later.

ABOVE: Even a small garden can accommodate a compost heap which will transform vegetable waste into a valuable soil conditioner.

OPPOSITE: A conservatory is a great way of adding elegant space to the house and at the same time moving living space into the garden.

Planning on paper

Take a digital picture of the garden from an upstairs window, reduce it to a relatively low resolution and print it out so that it fills a normal sheet of paper. Buy a few sheets of clear acetate film from the stationer's, and a wipe-off pen – perhaps two or three different colours.

Place a sheet of acetate film over the photograph of your garden and trace those existing features that are relevant – an existing path you want to or must retain, a manhole cover, perhaps the overhang of next door's sycamore tree. Mark the points of the compass as a guide to sunny and shady areas.

Take a second sheet of acetate, overlay it on the other one, then add your own ideas, drawn in very simply. Start with the patio and other paved and seating areas, then the conservatory, the shed and the paths. Adjust the shapes and areas if you need to by rubbing out with kitchen paper and redrawing.

When you have all the old and new basic features fixed, trace off a neat version in black, place it over the photograph, and lay another clean piece of acetate over the top so that you can experiment with your planning and planting ideas, using a different colour. First mark any areas of shade cast by trees inside or outside your garden, then choose an area for any special plants that you particularly like to grow, wherever suits them best. If there are no trees around the boundaries, or even if there are, decide on good places to plant one or two new trees. Don't forget to mark where their summer shadows will fall.

When you have your final version, with patio, paths, shed, conservatory, planting areas and trees marked in, photocopy the acetates to give you a permanent record of your plans. Don't forget that having photographed your garden from an angle, from an upstairs window, the perspective and scale will be a little distorted.

Planning on screen

The digital camera and the computer have made designing your own garden much simpler. If you're adept at using drawing or image manipulation software, start with the photograph from upstairs and adapt the view on screen to create a design before printing the final version. Easy-to-use design software is also available. This allows you to move the elements you need to incorporate around the plan and then present them in 3D so you can see how they will look.

Planning on the ground

In a brand new garden that is all lawn or all bare soil, planning on the ground can be simple and successful. Use a combination of posts, pegs, canes, boards, heavy-gauge twine and hosepipe to mark out your features on the ground exactly where they are to go.

A selection of 90cm/3ft and 1.8m/6ft canes, laid on the ground, can be used to mark straight-edged areas like patios and conservatories, and when these are decided upon, the canes can be replaced with pegs and string for more permanence. Use 1.8m/6ft canes or posts to mark sites for trees. Hosepipe is excellent for marking out curves (you may need to borrow extra from your neighbours). Laminated hose, being very flexible, is best for marking out the edges of beds, as it's easy to move slightly until positioned just where you want it. (It's also the best kind of hose for watering.) Choose a warm day if you can because the hose will be more flexible.

When you have the design fixed, it's not a bad idea to transfer the whole scheme to paper for a permanent record. Again, a photo from an upstairs window is often the simplest answer; one day your neighbours will want their hosepipes back.

This method can also be used in a relatively established garden where you intend to make few changes. Try to do it in winter when there's little foliage and top growth to get in the way.

Hiring a designer

This can be a chancy business, as there are some people who believe that taking a couple of one-day courses makes them qualified garden designers. Ask around

OPPOSITE: If your outdoor space is really tiny, you may be able to afford both a stylish design and high-quality timber and stonework.

among friends to find someone who's had their garden designed. Look at it, see if you think the design is successful and have a chat about the process – was the designer easy to work with and responsive? Gardening magazines may run design or planting services, but the design they provide is usually very basic.

Some garden centre chains also offer garden design services. These may comprise full garden plans or planting plans, sometimes with an additional construction service. It should not be difficult to get an idea of your local centre's reputation. Their designs are likely to be competent but unadventurous.

Finally, in the UK, you can go to the Society of Garden Designers. This is the professional society for designers of private domestic gardens, as distinct from larger-scale landscape designers. The society's website lists its members by county; you can be sure they will be professional in their approach. In the US, the Association of Professional Landscape Designers might be a place to start; you can search for members by state.

A few fundamental principles

Here are a few basic guidelines you should take into account when planning your garden.

- Don't put up with anything you don't like – change it.
- Do things the way you like them, even if others try to persuade you otherwise. Your garden should be as personal as your house.
- Plan for changing needs. Your young family may soon be grown up, your children may soon leave home, you may soon have less energy that you once did – keep these points in mind.
- Provide adequate paths for easy access.
- Make paths and plant trees first. Leave the fiddly bits till later.
- Take account of what's outside as well as what's inside the garden.
- Be sure the materials you use outside do not clash with the materials used in the construction of the house.

- Remember that shade can be as pleasant to sit in as sunshine.

Getting started

If you're new to gardening and indeed new to building, deciding where best to start can be difficult.

What to do first

If you're planning a conservatory or sunroom, have it built first. If you're planning to run the conservatory flooring out to make the patio, which is a great way of tying inside and outside into a cohesive whole, consider it one job. Do not erect a conservatory yourself. Next, lay paths – once you have good surfaces to walk on, everything else is so much easier. Even a simple gravel path that you might upgrade later will help enormously: your feet won't get muddy, the barrow will run more smoothly, materials are easy to move about – everything else takes half the time.

Next can come either the fences or the patio. Make the patio early on – it makes a good space to store materials off the wet ground (cover the patio with a sheet of polythene first, to prevent staining), and once you have a place where you can sit for your coffee break, you'll see the importance of privacy and want to get the fences up.

You can either put the barbecue and rubbish bin surround in place when you build the patio, or stack the materials and wait until later. If you'd like everything to match, buy the materials all at once; a later batch of what is supposed to be the same thing may turn out to be a slightly different colour when you go back to buy more.

If you wish, you can establish the whole of the rest of the garden as lawn and just eat into it with each new development. But if you're planning a concrete base for your shed, best get that over with at the same time as the patio and you won't need to hire a cement mixer again.

OPPOSITE: Blockwork paving in stripes of different colours can make the garden seem wider and also create a dramatic effect.

While all this construction work is going on, there's one more important thing that shouldn't be forgotten – weeds. They never stop growing, so they must be dealt with regularly either by using a non-persistent weedkiller, by regular hoeing or by digging out those weeds that have deep roots. That way they will never become a problem.

What to leave till later

All the fine details can be left till later. There's no point in buying delicate alpines and preparing special soil for them when you're surrounded by wheelbarrows and concrete. Hanging baskets will probably get in the way and be knocked off their hooks, bulbs will get trampled as they peep through the soil, and a row of parsley for the kitchen is unlikely to survive the comings and goings of all those boots and may well be accidentally hoed off with the weeds.

Planting trees

The only plants to think about putting in at an early stage are trees (or, more probably in a small garden, a tree), as they take a long time to mature. It's a good discipline to decide to plant your tree early, as it ensures that the rest of your plan is also carefully considered at an early stage, the positioning of trees having such an influence on the rest of the garden. Consider the possibility of purchasing a more mature tree if you want to create the impression of an established garden more quickly; you will find it a significant investment but one you may be willing to make, especially if it's the only tree in your small garden.

Plants from a previous garden

Most of us, when we move house, have favourite plants that we'd like to bring from our previous garden. And when moving into a first home, parents, relatives and friends are often generous with new plants and divisions

LEFT: If you find a well-established Japanese maple tree like this when you move into a new garden, you have acquired a most valuable asset - both in monetary terms and as a garden feature.

from their own gardens – often before we're ready to deal with them. But what do you do with them all when the garden is unprepared?

The answer is to prepare a small 'nursery bed', an area out of the way of all the comings and goings, perhaps simply fenced, where new plants can be set in rows for a year or so before being planted in their permanent homes. Anything can be transplanted happily a year after planting (many perennials will have grown enough to be split into two or three), so never be afraid to plant shrubs or border plants with the idea of moving them later – unless you're an unreconstructed procrastinator, in which case they will simply grow to maturity in the wrong place.

You may also spot attractive plants in nurseries, garden centres or catalogues. Rather than put off buying these for a year, a few can go in your nursery bed.

The pre-existing garden

Taking over an existing garden may prove to be a great relief or it may prove singularly frustrating. It's good to have an impressive tree without having to wait a decade for it to mature, but not if it casts so much dense shade that you can hardly see out of the back door. You may have been attracted to the garden by the delightful patio, but if it slopes back towards the house so that rainwater soaks the brickwork you may not think yourself so lucky. So while it's important to keep things going, it's also vital to assess coolly what you have.

Keeping things going

The first lesson is not to lose what you've taken over; if you let weeds invade and let the grass grow, it will take far more time to bring things back into order than if you looked after it all properly in the first place.

Lawn mowing

Keeping the lawn under control is vital for four reasons. First, if the lawn is cut, you won't feel guilty every time you look outside. Second, it will give you somewhere to sit out even if there's nowhere else. Third, sooner or later it will have to be cut, so it may as well look reasonable right from the start. And last, cutting the grass regularly keeps it healthy. This is important even if eventually you intend to dig some of it up.

The lawn may be long and lanky when you arrive – departing house owners are not well known for keeping their lawns neatly manicured. If you don't have a lawn mower, borrow one – new neighbours will surely sympathize and help with the loan of a machine. But if you intend to keep the grass, you'll soon need a mower of your own (see page 87).

Weeding

As in so many aspects of gardening, there's an old saying that applies here. Many of these words of 'wisdom' are out of date, even supposing they ever had any validity. This is the only one this book will repeat: 'One year's seeding is seven years' weeding.' The point being that once weeds have shed their seed, you'll spend the next seven years (and probably longer) pulling out the weeds that grow from that one batch of seed.

Think about removing weeds almost as soon as you arrive. If you do nothing else in your first year but cut the grass and weed the borders, you'll have had a constructive year.

When taking over an established garden, 'weeding' can mean anything from a little light hoeing to slashing through tangles of brambles. You can do it by hand, or you can use weedkillers and weed preventers to help do the job less arduously. Don't go heavy-handedly through the borders with a spade, as you will probably dig up perennials and bulbs that you would rather keep, and don't forget weeds in the lawn – these are easy to control with a feed-and-weed treatment.

Pruning

Only if branches from your own or neighbouring trees are hanging off dangerously will you need to pay attention to pruning. The only other plants that need concern you are bush roses and buddleias, which will

suffer if not pruned every spring. Cutting both back to about 23cm/9in in spring is an acceptable rough-and-ready rule for this first year.

Taking stock

Perhaps the first, very elementary, thing that ought to concern you is this: are there any hazards to you and your family and pets? Then, are there many plants in the garden? It's remarkable how sparse some people's gardens are. If your new 'established' garden really is sparse, you may be able to treat it as a completely new one – and go back to page 17!

General prospects

Many of the comments made in the section on assessing the soil in new gardens (see page 18) apply here, but in the case of an existing garden you have the extra complication of not knowing how well the previous owner has cultivated the soil. Some less thoughtful gardeners sow seeds, set plants and do nothing for them. Not only will their results have been poor, but when you inherit soil that has been treated in this way, it will need revitalizing. More thoughtful gardeners will have used both fertilizer and organic matter well, and in that case the soil should be in good heart.

It will usually be clear from the overall appearance of the garden if it is in good shape, and if the previous owners express interest in the degree of your own horticultural enthusiasm you can be pretty sure they feel they're leaving behind something worth having. If they ask to take one or two special plants with them when they move, so much the better.

Another clue: are there shrubs cluttered with dead branches? (Check in spring when the first leaves are appearing.) If so, you can bet that the other plants are similarly neglected.

Even in a well-cultivated garden the soil under the lawn may be poor – which you will discover if you dig it up to make changes. Organic matter is usually the

answer, combined with fertilizer, and in an old garden you may have the opportunity to create your own fairly quickly. Weeds may be present in great abundance and these will rot down to provide useful garden compost.

You will probably have considered the garden's compass aspect before buying the house but, if not, remember there are two sides to everything – a sunny patio at the back of the house where you can grow tubs of colourful summer plants means there must also be a shady place at the front where shade-loving plants should thrive. (See also page 206.)

There may be features of the garden or aspects of its layout that offend you straight away; change these as quickly as possible, as they're bad for your peace of mind. Others you'll only discover as you get used to the garden. You'll also find that the very fact that the paths, the shed and so on are in the positions that they are will itself wean you away from your first ideas for change. That's OK to some extent, but don't persuade yourself that you can live with your predecessors' ideas just because it involves less work.

Outside the garden

If the garden you're taking over is not new, there may be mature trees, large shrubs or even climbers encroaching from next door.

Trees may help shelter your garden from the wind, they may drop bullet-like walnuts into your pond, their leaves will undoubtedly collect in corners and the shade may or may not be welcome. Cooperate with your neighbour over any pruning – sometimes just removing one or two lower branches in their entirety can let in a great deal more light without spoiling the overall appearance of the tree.

If their tree is near your boundary, its roots will probably have grown into your garden and will be taking moisture and plant foods from your soil. This is more difficult to combat, but slates or corrugated iron sunk vertically into the ground along the fence line should keep many roots out; it's a rotten job, though.

Large shrubs can have a similar effect, and again discussion over pruning is usually the answer. You may

OPPOSITE: A wall is the best background of all for border planting and, in combination with a well-kept lawn, creates a superb traditional framework.

also find that shrubs planted some way from a fence on your neighbour's side have grown such stout branches that they're damaging the fence (see below). This will need urgent attention. Climbers, if left unpruned, can also weigh down a fence.

There is another side to all this. There may be eyesores outside the garden that you'd rather not gaze upon as you sit relaxing over a glass of wine. These can be masked by careful siting of trees, but in a small garden a tree large enough to blot out an office block may also cast black shade over virtually the whole plot.

One useful thing to remember is that a small tree planted nearer to where you sit will block out as much from your view as a large tree farther away. What's more, a tree at the edge of the patio will also provide valuable shade from the midday summer scorch.

There may also be views that you do not wish to obscure. The prospect of an ugly house or a tumbledown workshop may be more likely than a glimpse of green fields but, if the fields are there, planting trees that will obscure them is foolish. You can still plant a tree: a tall, narrow specimen tree can give you height and act as a focal point without blocking the view.

Fences and other timber

Although you may have inspected the various garden features when you viewed the house before buying, they rarely get proper attention. Once you've moved in, check them over.

Give the fences a good shake and lean on the posts; if pieces come away in your hand, at least you'll know it's vulnerable and won't be shocked when it collapses in a storm. If you fall into your neighbour's garden, the situation is serious. It may simply be that the panels are coming away from the posts, in which case new nails may be all that's required. You may find that the gravel board, which runs horizontally along the base of the fence as protection for the fence itself against rising soil moisture, is rotten and requires replacing.

If the posts themselves are rotten, you have two options. If the problem is below ground level, you can take fence and posts down, remove the rotten post stumps and re-erect the posts using steel post holders – the base of the post fits in at about ground level. If the problem is above ground, new posts will be required, and if the posts are in such poor condition, the panels may well also need replacing. Once the panels themselves start to fall apart, you're in rather more trouble, and although a certain amount of nailing

LEFT: A simple timber fence can be transformed into a striking feature by painting or staining it a dark colou r and training climbers into it.

and renewing battens can be worthwhile, there comes a point when replacement is the only option.

Pergolas and timber arches need much the same attention, but when it comes to trellis you may find repairs more difficult. Most trellis is fixed with steel staples at the crossing points, and once these corrode the whole thing starts to fall to pieces. Check the solidity of the fixings to the posts or wall, and if the crossing points are weak, a small screw in a pre-drilled hole will make a solid job of securing them.

Paving and paths

It's usually obvious if paths are cracked or patios collect the rain in puddles. What is less obvious is what's underneath, and this is important if you're considering heavy traffic or building on existing hard surfaces. Short of actually digging them up to see, the only way to find out how substantial the footings of paths and paved areas are is to excavate in the border or lawn alongside, so that you can see a cross-section of the way the footings are built up. You'll be surprised how many slabs are just laid directly on the soil; these will take only the lightest traffic.

If the footings are solid and there are still cracks in the path or patio, these may simply be due to poor pointing and renewing it should be sufficient. Once the water gets into the cracks and freezes, it makes them wider.

Concrete paths and patios that are in poor condition but that have good foundations can simply be topped with slabs, pavers or decking.

Greenhouses and other buildings

Floors and surrounds should be checked for cracks and subsidence in the same way as paths. Broken glass will be obvious – if the panes seem askew between the glazing bars, this may be a clue to subsidence. Check the state of the timberwork and probe carefully if you find any rot. Has it been regularly painted or treated with preservatives?

Old aluminium greenhouses are often the most difficult to repair. Manufacturers come and go, and finding replacement fittings that actually fit can be a headache; it's often simpler to take a ramshackle greenhouse down, get rid of it and start again from scratch. But don't do it straight away, as the limited protection that even a badly damaged greenhouse can provide for plants may prove valuable over your first winter in your new garden.

Finally, if you have any doubts about buildings, especially old outhouses that you may wish to use, consult a surveyor.

Trees

Some types of damage to trees are quickly visible. Exposed wood and damaged bark near soil level is a sign of thoughtless mowing or brushcutting. Check trunks for signs of wire having been tied around the tree; it may strangle the tree and kill it.

Look at your trees in winter: deciduous trees reveal the state of their branches when bare of leaves. You will be able to see those that are rubbing and causing wounds, cankerous patches, the red speckles of coral spot disease, splits in branches and bracket fungi. Early spring is a good time to remove branches of this sort.

Look again later in the spring, when the leaves are starting to shoot. This is the time when it's easy to see if any branches are dead. It's at this stage that you may discover that your tree is not worth keeping. You'll have to weigh up the value of a substantial tree that may not be as elegant as you would like after all the dead wood is removed, against the possibility of growing a new tree that will eventually be a better shape. The position of the tree and the importance of having another one in a different spot may tip the balance one way or the other.

Shrubs

Shrubs can be assessed in much the same way as trees – look for disease and damage in the winter and dead shoots in the spring. Then decide later if you actually like that particular variety; if not, take it out, however healthy it is. And do it at once, before you get too used to it. If you leave it in place, you may find that you cease to dislike it enough to remove it, but never like it enough to really appreciate it. Be tough.

Other plants

Plants such as perennials, bulbs and alpines are more tricky because, to put it bluntly, you can't always see they're there. You really need to give things a year to show themselves and for you to decide whether or not you like them. If the garden is a little neglected, some plants may put up a pretty poor show, but at least give them the chance to reveal their existence.

Some people have the urge to blast everything with weedkiller and start completely afresh, and I have sympathy with that approach. But old gardens often shelter mature and interesting plants that will flourish if given a little care and attention.

Making changes

It's unlikely that you'll like every single feature in your new garden, and most people will want to stamp their own personal touch on the garden anyway. You may have brought some favourite plants from your previous garden and need to find a new home for them, or you may wish to make more drastic alterations. Whatever the case, plan the changes carefully and in a logical order.

Making the garden your own

One of the themes of this section has been the very definite advice to make the garden your own – and to do it earlier rather than later. Make it reflect your own character and tastes, and that of your family, rather than allow yourself to be forced to follow the scheme that suited the previous occupant. I would even say that plants or features that you dislike should be removed as early as possible – even if you're not able to replace them at once. The resulting gap should inspire you to action.

Time, availability of funds, alternative priorities and enthusiasm will all govern how quickly you're able to work. The big things, those that offend you most, should be changed first and changed radically. Then the scene is set for you to add the details. Your motto should be: 'If in doubt, take it out.'

ABOVE: These cannas and cosmos, in brilliant and fiery colours, will create a dramatic display in the first season in your new garden.

OPPOSITE: Pebbles, laid in an unusually angular shape, help transform a simple small garden pond into a special feature.

Safety first

When it comes to safety, there are some areas that demand immediate attention. If you have large trees, inspect them carefully for damaged branches. It's not just storms and hurricanes that tear limbs from trees, and if there are branches partially torn off or caught in lower branches, they can come down at any time and cause damage or serious injury. If they overhang the pavement and injure someone when they fall, you'll be liable for compensation. If the branch is not accessible from a short, sturdy stepladder, get the professionals in to do it properly; choose a qualified tree surgeon.

Checking fences and paving will reveal any obvious safety problems, but you should also inspect ponds. This is vital if you have children, and perhaps even more so if you have friends with children who will be visiting – statistics show not only that children can drown in just a few centimetres or inches of water, but that more children drown in ponds when visiting friends than in their own garden. If it's at all likely that young children will be using the garden, drain the pond straight away. Covering it with plastic netting or erecting a low fence around it are just not good enough; kids have an alarming aptitude for getting where they want to go, however difficult you make it.

Having removed any aquatic plants, fish, frogs and other wildlife to a neighbour's pond (if you can't find a home for it all, contact your local wildlife organization), don't puncture the liner to allow the water to drain away but fill it with soil to make a bog garden. This can be planted with primulas and other bog plants and will make a lovely feature – unless it's in an inconvenient spot.

The alternative is to fill it with large pebbles or small rocks with no sharp edges to just above the water level. It will be wet but safe, as the water will be below the level of the stones. Marginal plants will grow in it well. When the children are older, the stones can be removed and the pond re-created. Either way, the look and atmosphere of the garden will be completely changed.

If you take over a large, captivating mature pool that's an integral part of the garden design, you will have to consider making it secure by using a temporary, but stout, high wire fence until the children are old enough to treat it responsibly.

Other safety hazards to be aware of include broken glass and sharp objects hidden in bushes, loose string and baler twine and, in urban gardens that back on to paths, needles. Just search the garden carefully.

Plants from your previous garden

Looking at your new garden, it may seem impossible to pick a place to plant the treasures that you've brought with you. Don't expect to be able to find them

permanent homes right away, but choose a spot – anywhere – that is fairly free of other plants and fork the soil over to remove all (and I mean all) perennial weeds. Mix in plenty of organic matter for all the plants except those that require good drainage, as this will encourage a fibrous root system that will help them when you move them again.

Don't worry about how you arrange them. Planting in rows is the best course because it makes weeding more straightforward.

Adapting a layout

The technique, described on page 26, of photographing the garden from an upstairs window and then using acetate sheets and non-permanent pens to try out changes works well with an established garden too, but it needs a little adaptation. Lay your first acetate over the enlarged photograph, then trace off those paths, paved areas, flowerbeds or other features and any specimen

ABOVE: An old shed can be integrated into the garden with climbers and annuals, and colour can be added with a window box.

OPPOSITE: Containers of hostas soften the lines of this cedar summer house and provide a range of foliage colours for many months.

trees or shrubs that you wish to retain and that are too big to move. Mark in the boundaries as well. Then put your original photograph to one side and place a new acetate over the first tracing. Try out your ideas in a pen of another colour on the clean acetate. When you've made your decisions, photocopy the two acetates together as before. Again, manipulating the image on the computer or using garden design software will produce a more sophisticated result.

Fitting in a shed

Some small gardens are too small for a shed – assuming you also want to sit in the garden and enjoy the scene. But if you have a family with bicycles or need a shed for DIY, a potter's wheel or your collection of atomic age umbrella stands, space must be found somehow.

Small lean-to stores in timber or steel are available that provide waterproof storage for a bicycle or a lawn mower and a few tools. There's also the ingenious solution of installing a low storage cupboard for bikes or bins that has a recessed area on top for planting, making it look more like a planter than a shed. If you need more storage space, however, a shed is the answer.

It always pays to buy a shed that is larger than you think you actually need. Then that little extra space will be there when you do need it – as you surely will. OK, we all know about Parkinson's law, but the fact is that there will always be things that need outside storage, and if the bicycles and tools take up the whole shed, you'll only regret not buying something a little larger.

Consider the site for your shed carefully. You don't want to have to wheel bikes through the whole of the garden, so site it as near the access as possible. Look for the shadiest, driest spot – the part of the garden least likely to appeal to plants – and consider this first. Under the overhanging branches of next door's sycamore is an excellent position for a shed.

RIGHT: Don't feel restricted to a run-of-the-mill shed or summerhouse; attractive windows and stylish colours can make it unique.

OPPOSITE: The light in a conservatory allows you to grow a wide variety of plants, but blinds are needed to help keep the room cool in summer.

If the shed is for a hobby or craft and you need electricity, a position nearer the house will save on the amount of cable you have to lay. Remember that you need a good path right to the door, so that you never get your feet muddy. Don't worry if you have to site the shed very near the house – put it to the side, near the back door if you like. It can be made to blend into the garden by covering it with climbers.

Conservatory

In a small garden a greenhouse is not practical unless you're a real enthusiast and are prepared to ensure that it's exposed to good light – which usually means it's exposed to view from the whole garden (and the house). So my vote goes to the conservatory,

a conservatory for living in, but perhaps with more plants than you would have in a room indoors.

The design needs careful consideration, as it should be big enough to be comfortable yet not so big as to dominate the garden. And you will have to take account of features and levels near the house that you wish to retain or that can't be altered. The smaller the garden, the less scope you have to make changes, especially in levels, and a little creative planning may be required.

It may be impossible to fit a standard conservatory into the space available, but many companies design and build conservatories to fit particular situations. This may be less expensive than you think, as the designers usually adapt relatively inexpensive standard components to a design that fits your individual circumstances. Choose a timber, paint finished, or natural or coloured aluminium structure to go with the style and materials of your house, and don't forget to think from the start about how it will relate not only to the house but also to the rest of the garden. Read too my thoughts on conservatories in new gardens (see page 23).

Lifting and re-using paving and bricks

Once you've investigated existing paths and paving, you may find that although the materials used are appropriate, they would be better used in a different way, or in a different part of the garden; most materials can be re-used. Even ugly concrete paths can be broken up and used as hardcore under a new surface.

Lift slabs or bricks carefully, always starting at the edge, and stack them out of the way. Paths made of bricks and concrete pavers are often edged with timber, which should be removed first. It pays to clean slabs or bricks well before re-using them; remove the worst of any remaining cement, then use a wire brush to finish up. Wear eye protection.

If you plan to plant or lay lawn over an area that has previously been paved, the soil will need forking over thoroughly to loosen it and let in air. The soil that has been under hardcore will also need forking over well.

Moving trees and shrubs

You may find you've inherited some specimen plants that you would like to retain but that are in the wrong place. What is possible and what is not are probably best summed up in these guidelines.

• You can move surprisingly large plants as long as you prepare well, move them carefully and then look after them.

• Large conifers are not easy to move, and other evergreens are also difficult. Deciduous plants are more likely to survive.

• Move conifers and other evergreens in early autumn or in spring. Deciduous shrubs can be moved at any time when they're without leaves and when soil conditions are good; late autumn and early spring are good.

LEFT: The much maligned crazy paving can be transformed by planting creeping plants to run steadily along the cracks.

OPPOSITE: One of the things you buy when you take over a mature garden is the time it took to develop; give it a season to see what bulbs and perennials emerge before deciding what changes to make.

- Always retain as much soil on the roots as possible.
- If possible, prepare the plants by cutting around them with a spade in the spring of the year before you intend to move them.

Think before you change

Taking over an established garden gives you one big advantage over moving to a brand new one – time, the time the plants have had to mature while your predecessor was in residence. So think twice before you throw that away, as it will take years to catch up. Large plants give a garden an air of maturity even if all around has been remade and replanted, so if you decide that substantial plants must go, it may pay to leave some of them for a few years until your other plants have had time to reach a substantial size.

Once you've decided to remove something, do it straight away; the sight of anything you find ugly will be continually offensive. But wait to install features that capture your enthusiasm until you have the time and resources to ensure that you can do a good job.

Quick fix

Your new garden, whether it be an established one or just a patch of earth on a new development, is going to need a lot of attention – not to mention the work you will be doing on the new house. While all this hard work is going on, it's very encouraging if you can arrange to have some attractive colour in the garden quickly.

Spring and summer seasonals

Seasonal plants (bedding plants) are those plants that flower for one season only and are then thrown away. They're among the most colourful of all garden plants

ABOVE: Annuals like these rudbeckias and nasturtiums can be bought in the garden centre in flower and will continue to bloom all summer.

OPPOSITE: Containers filled with bright annuals such as lobelia, marigolds and impatiens are an easy way to bring instant colour to a new garden.

and are ideal for small gardens; they can be bought from garden centres and DIY stores, usually in flower.

Spring seasonals include pansies, violas, polyanthus, wallflowers, forget-me-nots and double daisies, together with bulbs. These are sold and planted in the autumn for flowering in the spring or sold in spring in flower; some polyanthus and pansies will flower in the winter too, in areas where it's not too cold.

Summer seasonals are usually frost-sensitive and include geraniums, petunias, busy lizzies (*Impatiens*), begonias, marigolds, lobelia and alyssum. These plants are bought in late spring and summer and planted in the garden as soon as possible after the last frost in your area. Generally they flower until the first of the autumn frosts – sometimes beyond – although in poor soil and dry summers flowering may end prematurely.

Plants are sold in strips (six to ten plants in a long narrow tray), in packs (four, six or eight small plastic pots linked together to make a pack) or in individual pots. Strips and packs are the most economical, but plants in pots are larger and are usually sold in flower, so they make a more colourful instant display.

Seasonals can be used to fill a large empty bed for the most dramatic effect or set in spaces between other plants. The occasional plant can be slotted in wherever there's a gap, though large groups look better.

Soil for both spring and summer seasonals requires some preparation. Forking in a 5–7.5cm/2–3in layer of organic matter and scattering a handful of general fertilizer to the square metre or square yard before planting will give them a good start.

There's also an increasing enthusiasm for autumn seasonals, especially chrysanthemums. These are sold

in large pots in full flower and can create a colourful finale to the gardening year.

Containers

It's possible that there won't be the time to do anything in the garden except keep it ticking over. So containers, and especially tubs, may be the answer; avoid hanging baskets and window boxes at this stage, as they need too much looking after. Tubs can be sited where you most frequently pass – outside the front and back doors, by the front gate – and within sight of the kitchen and living-room windows. If you choose big containers, time spent caring for them will be limited.

You can splash out on beautiful tubs or urns that will fit well into your new garden, or you can buy cheaper, more functional ones. Large glazed or terracotta pots make wonderful house-warming presents, so drop a few hints before you move. Fill your pots with spring, then summer, then autumn seasonals, and also with bulbs.

Bulbs

The great thing about bulbs is that they're absolutely guaranteed to bloom; you have to do something drastic to prevent them from producing at least a small flower. This is because when you buy bulbs, most varieties already contain a miniature flower bud. They just need the right amount of moisture and warmth to flower beautifully, though without this warmth and moisture (if you leave the pack on the garage shelf, for example), flowers, of a sort, will still appear at the right season.

Spring bulbs are ideal companions for spring seasonals, and I would suggest that you use them in containers. Tulips are good growing through wallflowers; grape hyacinths are lovely among polyanthus or violas.

The term summer bulbs usually covers many plants – dahlias, for example – that are not bulbs in the botanical sense but are treated as if they are. Indeed, dahlias give perhaps the best value of all summer bulbs; they're easy to grow and produce vast quantities of flowers well into

LEFT: The tubs you bring with you from your previous house can immediately soften the lines at the front of your new home.

the autumn on big, bushy plants. Gladioli are flamboyant too, and begonias are probably the best summer bulbs for tubs – the trailing varieties are ideal hanging over the edge with taller, bushier plants behind them.

Quick-growing plants

In a brand new garden, quick-growing plants can make the garden seem mature in just a year or two – but what happens then? Some, like Leyland's cypress, just keep getting bigger and bigger, growing at 30–35cm/12–15in a year or more until you don't know what to do with them. Others are relatively short-lived plants that conveniently die on you, leaving a space for replanting.

Here are a few suggestions for plants that grow quickly. (See also page 234.)

Yarrow (*Achillea millefolium* – many varieties)
Feathery-leaved perennial with flat heads of flowers in a wide range of colours. Zone 2.

Wormwood (*Artemisia* 'Powis Castle')
Fine, silver foliage on a widely spreading bush. Zone 7.

Butterfly bush (*Buddleia* – many varieties)
Fragrant purple, lilac, pink or white flowers on an upright, arching shrub. Zone 6.

Californian lilac (*Ceanothus* 'Autumnal Blue')
Clouds of small blue flowers on an evergreen shrub. Zone 7.

Spotted dead nettle (*Lamium maculatum* – many varieties) Creeping perennial with foliage in combinations of green, silver and yellow plus red, pink or white flowers. Zone 3.

Tree mallow (*Lavatera* – many varieties)
Pink or white flowers on a spreading shrub with upright stems. Zone 8.

RIGHT: Tulips are inexpensive, easy to grow and guaranteed to flower; use them to provide colour and elegance for little outlay and effort.

Lupin (*Lupinus* – many varieties)
Flamboyant perennials, easy to raise from seed. Zone 4.

Tree Lupin (*Lupinus arboreus*)
Yellow lupin spikes on a rounded bush. Zone 7.

Gardener's Garters (*Phalaris arundinacea* 'Picta')
Creeping perennial with striped leaves. Zone 3.

Periwinkle (*Vinca major* 'Variegata')
Low stems with yellow-splashed leaves. Zone 7.

Chapter 2

Structural Features

In the end, it's the quality of the plants and the way they're arranged and grown that will determine the success or failure of a garden. But before you get as far as actually planting anything, get organized. For however impressive the planting, if the basic structure is not right, the plants will never be seen at their best. Boundaries are crucial - they define our own personal space, instantly set the style and highlight the opportunities. The patio and paths form an almost unchangeable framework, so plan carefully - and do you really need a lawn?

Boundaries

The best boundary you can have in a small garden is a wall, but building a new wall is prohibitively time-consuming and expensive, and unless you are lucky enough to move to a house that already has one, it is out of the question for most people. The choice you are left with is fences or hedges.

Fence or hedge?

A hedge is the least suitable choice for most small gardens. The hedge itself, when mature, will probably take up at least 60cm/2ft of valuable garden space, and you should allow another 45cm/18in for access and for the hedge's roots to suck up moisture and plant foods – as they will surely do – without depriving your border plants. Few gardeners do this. Hedges also take some years before they're large enough to do their job.

So this leaves us with fences, of which there are many types, in many materials and at many prices. They're less expensive and less solid than walls but need more maintenance; fences do not last as long as a hedge, but have no hungry roots; they take up less space than a hedge; and you can enhance the garden significantly by training shrubs, climbers or fruit on a fence.

Choosing a fence

Fences constructed of concrete panels are occasionally available, but are generally ugly and expensive, though more or less maintenance-free. Fences made of plastic vary enormously; some are ugly and can deteriorate surprisingly quickly. High-quality deer-fencing is tough and unobtrusive.

Chain-link wire fences are often provided on new developments, but may be only 60–90cm/2–3ft high. Ignore them when planning your new boundaries unless they're 1.2–1.3m/4–5ft high and noticeably stout. Taller chain-link fences, 1.8m/6ft high, at least keep dogs in or out. You can train climbers up them too, but

OPPOSITE: Rustic fencing can easily be constructed to your own design and here frames a view into the second part of the garden.

flimsier versions may sag under the weight of growth – and they never make the solid, comforting barrier that you need in a small garden when you may be sitting just a short distance from your neighbours. This leaves wood, the only practical choice for most gardens.

Timber fences come in a variety of styles and usually in panels in standard sizes. The timber used in fences is pressure-treated with preservative to give long-lasting protection against rot; its colour will fade over the years, especially on the sunny side.

Close-boarded

Overlapping, straight-edged vertical boards are fixed to horizontal rails. The toughest, most solid and soundproof barrier, it's also the most expensive. It does not usually come in panels, so it is the most laborious to erect.

Lapboard

This consists of horizontal, wavy-edged, overlapping boards in standard-sized panels. Generally solid and fairly soundproof, the boards will eventually warp.

Woven

These panels of thinner boards woven around vertical struts are less substantial, much less soundproof and have small gaps through which children like to peep.

Trellis

Trellis is an open arrangement of narrow timbers about 15–23cm/6–9in apart, making a square or diamond lattice. No barrier to sight or sound, trellis lets light through and provides good support for climbers. Trellis can be combined with other panels to provide light above a solid fence. Interesting and stylish designs are now available that are especially suited to town gardens.

Bamboo and wattle

Fences can be made of a variety of other timbers in various forms. Bamboo fences can be very attractive in a suitable setting, the canes set closely together vertically. Wattle hurdles make appropriate short-term fences in rural situations.

Erecting a timber fence

Timber fences are hung on stout posts, usually 1.8m/6ft apart, that are either sunk into the ground or set in steel post holders. About 60cm/2ft of the post should be sunk in the ground, so if the fence is to be 1.8m/6ft high, for effective privacy, you need 2.4m/8ft posts. For a 1.8m/6ft fence, the posts should be 10cm/4in in diameter; for a 1.2m/4ft fence, 7.5cm/3in posts will do.

The simplest method of setting posts is to use a post-hole borer, which digs out a hole just a little wider than the post itself. This can be hired. The narrow space left after the post is inserted is then packed tight with soil. To ensure that most of the water is kept away from the post and so increase protection against rotting, it's better to dig out a hole larger and deeper than is required. Put some gravel or crushed hardcore in the bottom, set the post in at the correct height, then fill up to the top with more gravel, ramming as hard as possible as you go. (Keep this gravel weed-free.) Alternatively, after the hardcore is rammed in, fill the hole with a runny concrete mix.

Post holders are a useful alternative. A post holder consists of a long, steel, flanged spike, with a socket at the top to take the foot of the post. This socket may be adjustable to enable you to ensure that the post is vertical. The post holder is simply knocked into the ground with a sledgehammer, then the post is fitted in the top, adjusted until vertical and tightened well. Post holders are impractical in rocky soil because the spike tends to be forced out of alignment as it's knocked in.

To erect a fence, first secure the help of a friend or neighbour. Next, use your garden line to mark the line of the fence. Erect the first post, checking that it's vertical by using a spirit level. Nail the first panel to the first post, holding a brick behind the post to take the force of the blows. Be sure it's level; your helper can support the other end.

LEFT: Attractive timber fencing can be made to your own design and painted any colour you like.

OPPOSITE: The well-spaced lines of a picket fence look just right bounding an intricate planting of mainly evergreen perennials.

You can now mark the position of the next post, swinging the panel slightly to one side to give yourself enough room to set it. The panel can then be swung back into position and nailed in place.

Continue in this way to the end of the run. If you find that the length of your boundary is not an exact multiple of the width of your panels, dismantle the framework at the end of the last panel, saw the boarding to the appropriate length, rebuild the framework and nail it in place.

Finish by nailing weather caps on the tops of the posts to prevent water from soaking into the endgrain and encouraging rotting.

Staining a fence

All ready-made panels are pre-treated with preservative and usually come in a pale orange-brown or a richer brown shade that becomes paler as it weathers. But a wide range of coloured preservatives and stains is now available that will colour outdoor timber to your preferred shade and can look very stylish. They're especially effective in a tiny garden or small yard.

Supporting plants

Climbers and wall shrubs grown on walls and fences need support. With trellis you simply tie your plants to the struts, but other fences, and walls, need to be provided with a means of securing the plants.

Fences

Screw 7.5cm/3in steel eye-screws into the end posts at right angles to the fence line and at 30cm/12in intervals, starting 30cm/12in above ground; use smaller rings for the other posts and the central strut of each panel. Fix straining bolts into the rings in the end posts, with the eyes facing along the fence. Twist galvanized wire tightly on to one eye, thread the wire through the rings at the end of the fence, then tie to the last bolt. Tighten the nuts at both ends to tension the wire.

Walls

Drill and plug holes before fitting rings and wire as for fences.

Choosing hedging plants

Even if your garden is large enough to cope with hedges, it still pays to choose your hedging plants carefully. The last thing you want is to be forced into cutting a hedge all the time when you've more important things to do – like lazing in the sun.

Lists of hedging plants for different purposes can be found on page 209. Leyland's cypress is best avoided in a small garden unless you love hedge trimming; never fall ill, for it grows very quickly (up to 90cm/3ft a year),and needs a great deal of attention to keep it from getting out of hand, so be warned. Privet is also a mistake, for although it can make a neat hedge, its roots are shallow, widely spreading, greedy and thirsty, and plants growing nearby suffer greatly. If in doubt, go for a yew hedge, unless you plan to move in a year or two.

Planting a hedge

The technique for planting a hedge is the same as for planting a single shrub (see page 102), except that the whole process is linear. Your hedge will be in place for many years and you'll be constantly stimulating its growth by pruning, so the site needs good preparation.

Start by marking the edge of the hedge line on the neighbour's side, 30cm/12in from the boundary, with a garden line (see page 93). Dig a trench 30cm/12in wide along your side of the line. Make it as deep as your spade and pile the soil along your side. Spread organic matter in the bottom of the trench 5–7.5cm/2–3in deep and fork it in. Mix the same amount of organic matter with the soil you've excavated, then put the whole lot back into the trench and tread it well. Leave the surface of your trench 2.5–5cm/1–2in below the level of the adjoining border; spread the surplus soil on the border.

Stretch the garden line along the middle of the prepared area. Using a measuring stick (see page 93), set out the hedging plants in a single row at the appropriate spacing (see page 56) and plant them with a spade or a trowel according to their size. The depression along the length of the trench allows you to water them in easily.

Follow the same approach when planting hedges within the garden – as structural features and around a potager or herb garden, for example.

RIGHT: Rectangular brick pavers edged with box plants trimmed into spheres create an interesting contrast of clean lines.

OPPOSITE: A warm-coloured wall makes the perfect background for a fruit tree trained on wires.

Spacing hedging plants

It is important to space the hedging plants you choose at the appropriate distance, depending on the spread and rate of growth of the particular plant.

Box (*Buxus sempervirens*) As a boundary hedge 45cm/18in; as a low edging hedge use 'Suffruticosa' 12.5cm/5in

Hornbeam (*Carpinus betulus*) 45cm/18in

Lawson's cypress (*Cupressus lawsoniana* 'Green Hedger') 45cm/18in

Escallonia (*Escallonia* 'Donard Radiance') 60cm/2ft

Beech (*Fagus sylvatica*) 45cm/18in

Holly (*Ilex aquifolium*) 45cm/18in

Privet (*Ligustrum ovalifolium*) 30cm/12in

Firethorn (*Pyracantha*) 45cm/18in

Rose (*Rosa* 'Iceberg') 60cm/2ft; *R. rugosa* 90cm/3ft

Rosemary (*Rosmarinus* 'Miss Jessopp's Upright') 60cm/2ft

Snowberry (*Symphoricarpus* 'White Hedge') 45cm/18in

Yew (*Taxus baccata*) 45cm/18in

Western red cedar (*Thuya plicata* 'Atrovirens') 60cm/2ft

Viburnum (*Viburnum tinus* 'Eve Price') 45cm/18in

Maintaining hedges

You will need to carry out regular maintenance on your new hedge. Most hedging plants are best cut back by half immediately after planting, to encourage them to make a dense hedge. The following year, cut them back by a third, and cut them back by another third each year until their final height is reached. Make sure they're well watered, especially in their first summer.

After they reach their final height, hedges are best cut to leave their profile slightly narrower at the top than at the base; a flat top is easier to cut evenly than a rounded one. Cut hedges regularly; if left uncut for too long, they become thin, sparse and ineffective as boundaries.

ABOVE: Low box hedging can be planted in intricate patterns to create an attractive structure that provides interest all year round.

LEFT: Beech makes an excellent garden hedge, especially as the leaves tend to stay on the plant all winter, passing from this attractive butter yellow to a warm brown.

Paths and driveways

After the boundaries, the patio, sitting area and paths should be your next priority. The ability to keep your feet dry and mud-free from early on is a great incentive to use the garden, even in winter, and makes the addition of winter plants all the more valid. Paths do not necessarily have to be permanent. You can use temporary materials for temporary paths, then after a year or two you can make adjustments and make them permanent.

Siting paths and drives

You're unlikely to have a choice about the route of the drive to a garage or parking area. But you can make a drive seem less obtrusive in a relatively small front garden by making the whole area into a gravel garden. Set solid foundations under the area that the car is to use – perhaps with some large stones inset along the edge for guidance – and when the car is not there, the drive will simply look like an open area in the gravel garden.

Paths need to be both functional and decorative. The overall garden layout will dictate the line of the paths, but even in the small garden you should try to avoid dead ends – if you can walk round in a loop rather than just down the path and then back again, it makes even going to the dustbin interesting.

In a very small garden, a single loop of path with borders at the sides and an area of grass, gravel, paving or more planting in the centre is simple and effective. The bins, barbecue and shed can all be set to the side so that the same path gives access to them all. The central area could even be paved as a patio, so that in effect the path runs round the margin of, and merges with, the patio. The path could be picked out in a different but complimentary material, or the same material could be chosen but in a different colour.

RIGHT: Reconstituted stone paving, boulders, pebbles and timber – together with plants, of course – combine to bring interest and style to a simple situation.

Straight paths are awkward, unless you wish to use them to distort the perspective. A straight path that narrows slightly towards the far end will make a small garden look longer, but a long straight path parallel to a boundary can look dull unless the whole design of the garden is formal. Edged with low box hedging, a straight path can make a stylish feature, but don't bisect a small garden with a central path unless the whole garden is intentionally broken into smaller formal areas – run it closer to one side. Paths made of individual stones set in grass are old-fashioned and are fiddly to maintain. Avoid large precast concrete footprints.

Choosing materials

Choosing the right material for paths and patios is probably more important than choosing sympathetic walling or fencing, as they are not going to be covered

with plants. Your choice will be governed not only by the material used in your house walls but also by size of garden, price, ease of laying and the importance of permanence.

Brick

Brick is one of the best choices. The scale is right, and bricks weather to give such an attractive finish. Bricks can be mystifying in their variety, but whatever you choose must be frost-resistant, otherwise the surface will break up after winter weather. Second-hand bricks from salvage yards give an instantly mature look and come in a variety of muted colours.

Concrete pavers

Similar in scale to bricks, these come in interlocking angular shapes as well as the usual rectangles. The colour range is less wide and the individual shades and colours are more uniform. Concrete pavers are ideal in association with new houses and, if chosen carefully, also look good around older properties.

Stone slabs

Mellow and elegant, stone slabs are also expensive, and may come in large sizes that can be heavy and difficult to handle. But they're perfect for larger areas and alongside stone house walls.

Reconstituted stone slabs

These can be surprisingly effective, especially as many of them contain a large proportion of ground stone. They sometimes resemble riven stone and, as they come in more manageable sizes and at a more manageable price, they're deservedly popular.

Setts

Small square setts, usually granite, are very attractive but expensive. They're fiddly to lay and their uneven surface can cause problems. Prefabricated slabs made up of a series of 'setts' are now available in various patterns and are laid just like slabs, to give a sett-like finish that is only about 2.5cm/1in deep.

Cobbles

Cobbles, or DTs (dogs' testicles! as they're known in the British landscape trade), are very uncomfortable to walk on, so they are useful as an edging or as a boundary between a path and an area where you wish to discourage people from walking.

Concrete

Straightforward concrete laid on site is inelegant as a final surface and should be avoided, but such pads are often necessary under buildings or under drives that will be taking heavy loads.

Gravel

A very useful and inexpensive surfacing, gravel is more suitable for informal areas than patios. But it's ideal where paths can merge into beds, which can also be gravelled to keep down weeds. It also makes fine, relatively inexpensive, short-term surfacing.

Bark chips

You can use bark chips in a similar way to gravel; they're especially good as paths in shade and are ideal as surfacing for children's play areas.

Timber

Decking is sweeping the country, and even the Royal Horticultural Society now recommends it. It looks especially good in small areas, as a patio surrounded by a gravel garden, perhaps. It can either be used to help create harmony in a garden with timber fences or, stained brightly, to harmonize with housepaint and even outdoor tiling.

A handy DIY person can easily build a good deck from pressure-treated timber or specially cut deck boards (which are often fluted to reduce slipping), but it needs careful construction and attention to the levels. For the less expert, pre-built decking 'slabs' are also

OPPOSITE: The combination of hard surfaces and plants is crucial to the look of the garden; here, silver and grey foliage nestle under the blue-green euphorbia alongside lookalike York stone slabs.

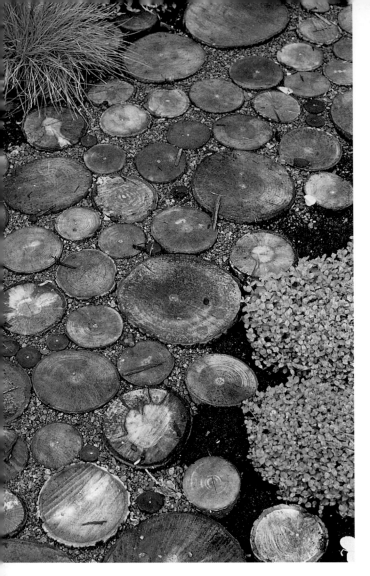

available and are ideal for simply butting side by side over an old concrete patio.

Mixing materials

By mixing materials thoughtfully you can create some very interesting effects, and also deal imaginatively with the transition from one area of the garden to another. Stone and brick, stone and gravel, brick and gravel, two different-coloured bricks, timber and bark – all look good together if the colours are chosen well.

Preparing the site

The way in which a site is prepared before the surfacing is laid depends partly on the eventual surface but also on the traffic it's going to carry – an occasionally used path needs less in the way of foundations than a drive that will be taking the weight of a car.

Paths

An occasionally used path made of brick or concrete pavers or of rough stone can be laid on well-compacted soil, but the addition of 2.5cm/1in of sand will help to bed it in. A layer of landscape fabric under the sand will prevent weeds from coming through. Lay bark chips straight on landscape fabric.

Footpaths in brick, concrete pavers or small slabs can be laid on compacted soil plus 2.5cm/1in of sand, but paths taking regular heavy loads – motorbikes, for example – are best laid on a sub-base of 7.5cm/3in of compacted hardcore topped with 5cm/2in of sharp sand.

Driveways

The additional stress caused by the regular use and extra weight of the family car(s) calls for a very solid construction. Start with 15cm/6in of compacted hardcore on a firm soil base; ensure that all crevices are filled with dry sand. Next lay 5cm/2in of sharp sand and then your brick, paver or slab surface.

It always pays to err on the side of extra stability and, for drives, 10cm/4in of hardcore and then 5cm/2in of concrete topped with slabs is probably the most reliable option, although if bricks or pavers are laid well and vibrated into place thoroughly they will take the weight.

Laying a path or drive

Again, the way in which a path or driveway is laid will depend both on the material being used and the traffic the structure will carry.

Brick

For paths that don't have to take the weight of a car, make sure the site is level and is excavated to a depth of 12.5cm/5in, plus the thickness of the bricks, after ramming firm. Edges that don't abut walls or another

ABOVE: Logs in different sizes, treated with preservative, make an interesting path, especially when set off by glass beads laid among them.
OPPOSITE: Gravel paths provide structure, texture and a good foil for plantings. They can be enlivened by the use of interesting 'stepping stones'.

solid vertical surface need edging to keep the bricks in place. Use 7.5cm/3in wide, 2.5cm/1in thick pressure-treated softwood planks (which can be stained in a colour of your choice), held in place from the outside by 5 x 5cm/2 x 2in posts knocked in well below the eventual finished level.

Start by putting in 7.5cm/3in of hardcore, roughly levelled and well rammed down. Fill any crevices with sand, then spread 5cm/2in of dry sharp sand and level it off neatly with a plank. Decide on the basic pattern of bricks, then start to lay the bricks, working from a board – never stand on the sand. Don't worry about filling odd angles as you go along – finish laying the whole bricks and then fill the odd spaces with pieces of brick, cut using a bolster and hammer or an angle grinder (wear protective goggles). The bricks should end up about 10mm/⅜in above the final level.

When you've finished laying the bricks, use a hired plate vibrator to work them down firm, then spread some sharp sand over the surface and brush it in. Finally, go over all the bricks with the plate vibrator to settle the sand in the cracks.

For a driveway that will carry cars, use 15cm/6in of hardcore and 5cm/2in of sharp sand. For extra stability, brush in a dry mortar mix of 1 part cement to 3 parts sand.

Concrete pavers

Concrete pavers come not only in the usual rectangular format but also in a variety of more angular shapes. The range of colours is more limited. Lay them in the same way as bricks.

Stone and concrete slabs

These are laid in the same way as bricks, but for extra support they can be set on five spots of mortar rather than simply laid on sand. Use a fist-sized dollop of mortar (1 part cement to 4 parts sand) in each corner of the slab and another dollop in the middle. For drives that will have to take the weight of a car – or heavier vehicle – lay a 5cm/2in thickness of concrete over the whole area.

Setts

These are bedded in sand in the same way as bricks, but make sure you allow for the extra depth when calculating the depth of your excavations. Their shape will prevent you from using a plate vibrator to settle them in.

Cobbles

These can be laid loose but are better laid in a mortar mix. Start with 7.5cm/3in of compacted hardcore, then add 5cm/2in of dry concrete mix. Set the cobbles packed close together in the dry mix with about half the cobble exposed. Finally, lightly sprinkle the whole area with a spray of water to harden the concrete and wash the concrete off the pebbles.

Gravel

For drives, a good base is needed to prevent cars from churning up the gravel. Start with 10cm/4in of rammed hardcore, then 5cm/2in of coarse gravel mixed with sand. Roll this flat, then top with 2cm/¾in of pea gravel, raked level and rolled in. It's essential to provide an edging of brick or boards where there's no existing solid boundary, otherwise the gravel will creep into the border or on to the lawn. For paths, taking much lighter loads, a 2.5cm/1in layer of gravel over landscape fabric laid on compacted soil retained by a firm edging is sufficient.

Bark

Bark can be laid in the same way as gravel, although a greater depth, say 5cm/2in, is usually advisable.

Mixing materials

The big problem with mixing materials, especially when using different slabs and bricks, is the variation in thickness. The best approach is to prepare your base for the thickest materials and then add extra firmed sand or mortar to support the thinner ones.

OPPOSITE: Reclaimed bricks bring an instant look of maturity to a new path, but it's important to choose frost-resistant types.

Patios and sitting areas

The patio or terrace is a place to sit and relax, to eat and to party. In a small garden there's not always much choice as to its siting, but the time when you'll use it most and the uses to which you'll put it should dictate its position.

Location

If you like to relax outside in your garden after a day's work, a west-facing site will give you the best light and warmth at that time. Bear this in mind when devising your planting scheme for the west of the patio site. If you use the patio mainly at weekends for lunching, maybe with friends, it's important that it should be sufficiently spacious and get plenty of midday sun, although shade is also increasingly welcome.

If the back of the house faces south or west, this is the obvious place for the patio. If you need to site it farther down the garden, try to choose an area as near the house as possible, or add one or two small paved areas, with space for a chair or two, where you can just nip out for ten minutes with the paper.

Materials

Always consider the house, the garden and other surfaces when choosing 'hard' materials. Gravel and bark are usually suitable only for a sitting area; they're simply not firm enough to take chairs and tables. Bricks, concrete pavers, stone, the more stylish concrete slabs and decking are ideal.

Preparing and laying the patio

Use the same techniques as for laying a path or drive (see page 60) – 7.5cm/3in of hardcore on compacted soil plus 5cm/2in of sharp sand will give a solid base to support regular use.

Using decking

Treated timber planks make an attractive, long-lasting and natural surface, although laying them involves more than simply nailing down boards. Posts are

required to support a framework of joists, and the boards are then screwed to the joists in a diagonal or right-angle pattern.

Squares of treated timber decking can be bought at some garden centres and DIY stores. These are fitted together like paving stones and are useful for small areas. Consult the manufacturer's literature for details of how to use them.

Various composite and synthetic materials are increasingly being used to build decks, and these can be very stylish and are especially valuable in modern settings. They are often more durable than timber and, of course, do not diminish natural resources in the same way. These alternatives, often composed of recycled plastics and timber, may be designed to resemble real wood or may make no such attempt. They usually require minimal maintenance but do not have the structural performance of timber and therefore are not used for joists. Vinyl, stainless steel and aluminium are also sometimes used as decking materials; these need specialized fixtures and supports.

Decking is a convenient way of creating a level sitting area on a sloping or very uneven site. It looks good with water, requires only occasional maintenance, and is a soft and natural way of linking house and garden together. But the decking must be solidly built or it will sag and may become slippery, especially after rain and in shady situations. For anything other than a simple plan, it pays to consult a joiner while still at the planning stage. It looks easy on the TV, but it can still be very tricky if you've never done it before.

Preparation

First, be sure that the area to be covered with decking is free of perennial weeds or they'll be fighting their way through the boards. Level off roughly, allowing a slope away from the house, then lay a sheet of

ABOVE: This mixture of surfaces may be less straightforward to lay than slabs, but looks delightful with the thymes spilling over.

OPPOSITE: Even a small, inexpensive area of deck with some basic furniture can make a lovely place to sit out in the sunshine.

landscape fabric over the soil to prevent more weeds from emerging, and cover the fabric with 5cm/2in of gravel.

Choosing timber

Hardwoods last the longest, and do not always need treating with preservative, although it still pays in the long run. Be careful of any wood treated with chromated copper arsenate (CCA), which contains toxic arsenic, copper and chromium compounds. Be sure to buy timber from managed plantations; it should be so marked. Oak, teak, iroko, opepe and jarrah are all suitable for decking. Softwoods are significantly cheaper and often more readily available, but need pressure treatment before use and may still not last as long as hardwoods.

4 x 4in), wooden joists (150 x 50mm/6 x 2in), building blocks to support posts, ballast and cement, bolts to support the frame, joist hangers, and stainless steel or brass countersunk screws.

Construction

A deck is built by constructing a frame supported on blocks and joists to which the boards are fixed.

First mark out the area for your deck, using the set square to be sure the corners are at true right angles – unless you prefer a fancier design. The posts must go at the corners and 1.5m/5ft apart around the edge on longer runs; mark their locations. At each point where a post is to go, dig out a hole 30 x 30cm/12 x 12in and as deep. Place a building block in the bottom of each hole.

Set a post vertically in each hole (cut each to be a little longer than the eventual height of the deck), check with a spirit level to be sure each is absolutely upright, then fill the hole with concrete. Be sure to pack it tightly. Do them all, then leave the concrete to set for two days.

When the concrete is set, attach the joists to the outside of the posts with bolts, then attach joists across the area of the deck every 30cm/12in using joist hangers. Keep checking with the spirit level to be sure the level is right. Cut off the tops of the posts with a power saw level with the frame.

Screw the boards to the joists at 45° or 90° to the joists, pre-drilling the holes and leaving a small gap of about 10mm/⅜in between the boards. Use your garden line to mark the edge, then, using a power saw, cut off all the protruding edges, leaving an overlap of 5cm/2in. Treat all cut surfaces with preservative.

Finally, paint or stain the whole thing in the colour of your choice.

Boards come in a variety of widths: 75–150mm/ 3–6in; the bigger the deck, the wider the boards should be. Grooved boards are less slippery in the wet but are not to everyone's taste.

Tools and materials

You'll need an electric drill, power saw, screwdriver, set square, spade, spirit level and tape measure. You'll also need decking boards, wooden posts (100 x 100mm/

ABOVE: This patio makes use of a mixture of materials and shapes - square-pattern paving, diamond trellis, rounded containers and pebbles - rather than elaborate planting, to create interest and texture in the garden.

OPPOSITE: Fluted timber boards minimize slippage in shady areas and the weathered colouring is offset by flowers and white-variegated hostas.

The lawn

Why have a lawn in a small garden? It's fine to have a lawn if you like the look of grass to offset plants, but remember this – the lawn will get a great deal of concentrated wear and will be difficult to keep looking good. In a small garden, where the lawn is always right in front of your eyes, it really does need to look impressive.

Pros and cons

Mowing a small area is fiddly and you need a decent lawn mower to do a good job – plus somewhere to keep it, and a power point. In addition, as our summers

ABOVE: Turf comes in easy-to-lay rolls, gives an instant effect and is available in different grades for different situations.

OPPOSITE: A small space does not have to be formal; grasses and boards create a comfortable but naturalistic atmosphere.

become warmer and drier, the lawn needs regular watering to keep it looking green. And is watering the lawn a reasonable use of purified drinking water? In some places it's actually illegal. Finally, the horticultural reason for abandoning the lawn: if you fill a substantial area with grass, there will be much less room for interesting plants.

So, you get the message: in general I'm against making a lawn in a very small garden. In some situations, however, a lawn can be very effective in creating a setting for plants. It can provide space for restrained games and for relaxing, and it will certainly create a naturally verdant atmosphere.

Turf or seed?

There are two ways of establishing a lawn – you can sow seed or you can lay turf.

Turf:
- is more expensive;
- gives a green finish straight away;
- can be walked on soon after laying;
- gives a guaranteed even finish if laid well.

Seed:
- is cheaper;
- needs more care to create an even finish;
- is available in a wider variety of types for different situations;
- cannot be walked on for many months;
- needs good care in the early stages.

In a small garden, where you won't need all that much, my advice is always to go for turf. But don't just buy it on spec from an advertisement in the local paper. Buy specially grown, cultivated turf that is raised specifically for gardens from selected seed and is weed-free. It will be absolutely even in thickness, so if you've prepared a level surface, your lawn will end up level. Turf bought through an advert in your local paper may well be stripped from fields, full of coarse grasses and weeds, and not evenly cut.

If you grow your lawn from seed, you need the time to prepare well and look after the lawn carefully in its early stages.

Preparation

Preparation is much the same whether you use turf or seed. Fork over the area to the depth of a digging fork, then spread 5–7.5cm/2–3in of organic matter over the surface and fork it in. If the soil is heavy and sticky, 2.5–5cm/1–2in of grit forked in will also be helpful. It's best to do this preparation before you plant the borders, so that you can spread any spare soil there.

After forking, the whole area needs treading (see page 101); if it's not firmed well, it may sink unevenly later. Now carefully rake it level, removing any large stones or lumps of organic matter. If you find that it is rather uneven, rake soil from the heights to the hollows but then tread the refilled hollows before raking level again.

The next job is to spread a pre-sowing fertilizer as recommended on the pack and to rake it in evenly. This will stimulate root growth and give seed or turf a good start.

Ideally it pays to prepare the soil and rake it level some weeks before you apply the fertilizer and sow the seeds. Any weeds then have a chance to germinate and can be hoed off or treated with weedkiller and so cause much less trouble later.

Sowing seed

Grass seed can be sown in spring or autumn. In the autumn you have fallen leaves to contend with, and these can smother young seedlings. In spring there's the risk of drought when the grass seedlings are young, so you must water them. I favour early autumn, if only because there are so many other things to do in the spring. If you find that you have to sow when the soil is dry, water well, using a sprinkler, after preparation and about a week before you intend to sow.

Grass seed comes in mixtures, each for a different use and each blend being specially formulated from a variety of different types of lawn grass for an individual situation or purpose. So you will find hard-wearing

mixtures, mixtures for shade, fine-leaved mixtures for the most elegant lawns and so on. Choose the mixture that suits your purpose.

When you come to sow your grass seed, you'll need a number of 1.2m/4ft and 1.8m/6ft canes, as well as your measuring stick, a paper cup, a felt-tip pen and kitchen scales. The pack will tell you the amount of seed to put on each square metre or square yard of soil. Weigh this amount on the scales and tip it into your paper cup. Shake it so that the surface of the seed is level, then mark the level it reaches on the inside of the cup with the pen.

Next, lay long canes end to end down one side of the area to be sown, and lay another row parallel, a metre or yard away. (You can use your garden line for this if you don't have enough canes.) Finally, use 1.2m/4ft canes to mark off your metre- or yard-wide strip into square metres or yards.

To sow the correct amount of seed, use one cup filled up to the marked level for each square. Simple. To help ensure even coverage, sprinkle about half the seed over the square, working from side to side, then go over the same area again, working from top to bottom. Then move on to the next square. When the whole plot is done, remove the garden line and canes

ABOVE: Making a new lawn from seed depends on even application, and it pays to keep fallen leaves from smothering the newly emerged grass.

OPPOSITE: A lawn surrounded by paving with borders at the edges sounds dull but looks elegant, allows good access and provides a feeling of spaciousness.

and rake over gently to mix the seed into the surface of the soil.

Birds can be a big problem on newly sown lawns – they not only eat the seed but also take dust baths in the fine soil. Prevent this by covering the area with fine-mesh plastic netting, simply laid on the soil and secured with a few stones around the edge.

If the soil dries out after sowing, you may need to water – use a fine sprinkler and give it a good soak.

Caring for newly sown lawns

A couple of weeks after sowing, a green haze will start to appear and will become greener and greener; weeds will appear too. Remove the plastic netting when the grass is about 2.5cm/1in high, and when it's about 5cm/2in high it can be cut for the first time. Use a cylinder or a wheeled rotary mower if you can, and collect the mowings in the grass box. Cut it to about 2.5cm/1in in height. For autumn-sown lawns this may be the last cut of the year, but spring-sown lawns should then be cut every week or ten days, gradually lowering the height of the cut to about 12mm/½in by July.

It's important to deal with weeds as early as possible, but if weedkillers are used when the grass is still young, they may cause damage. Annual weeds will be killed by mowing; isolated perennial weeds can be carefully dug out by hand while still small. You may need to use a weedkiller if your weed problem is severe, but check the advice on the packs to find one that is suitable for a new lawn. In the meantime, use spot treatment.

Try to keep off the lawn for at least three months, except when mowing, and preferably for longer.

Laying turf

Turf can be laid at any time of the year when the soil is not parched, frozen or waterlogged. It follows that spring and autumn are usually best.

Like grass seed, specially grown turf comes in a number of grades that are suitable for different purposes. Your turf will be delivered in rectangular pieces, which are usually rolled up for easier carriage. Turf from meadows is usually 90 x 30cm/3 x 1ft; specially grown turf usually comes in larger pieces. Stack it in a shady place and spray it over with water if you're not able to lay it at once.

When you come to lay the turf, you'll need a stout plank, a rake, an old kitchen knife and some used but not lumpy sowing or potting compost. Start by unrolling turves end to end around the edge of the area to be turfed. Use an old kitchen knife to cut

RIGHT: Lawn edging helps to separate grass from the gravel, and if its design is interesting, can be a feature in itself.

OPPOSITE: A lawn can be used to create a still pool of green and a relaxing air when surrounded by lots of detail.

the ends to fit and when you go round corners. Tap them into place using the flat of the rake.

Now place your board along the edging row of turf and work from it without treading on either the newly laid turves or the prepared soil. The board helps spread your weight. Starting in one corner, unroll more turves across the plot from one side to the other in a straight line. Cut the ends of the turves to fit accurately, but do not attempt to bend them to match any curves in the parallel edge – just leave some narrow gaps for the time being.

When the first row is done, move the board across, cut a turf in half and lay that at the start of the next row. Then continue with full-sized turves as before. The purpose of starting with a half-turf is to ensure that the joins between turves do not coincide. Continue in this way across the plot. You'll probably be left with a long, fairly narrow gap at each end, and some spare turves and offcuts. Use these to fill the gaps, but try to use the largest possible pieces, as large pieces are less likely to move. Don't make a patchwork of small bits.

Clear away any mess, then sprinkle the used potting compost lightly over the whole area – not more than half a bucketful to the square metre or square yard. Using the back of the rake, work it into the grass, paying special attention to the joins between the turves. Finally, water well, using a lawn sprinkler.

Caring for newly laid turf

Your newly turfed lawn will probably need mowing in a couple of weeks. Again, use a cylinder or wheeled rotary mower with a grass box, and cut it to about 2.5cm/1in. If the turf has been laid in spring, it may need watering regularly until the roots have penetrated well. You will be able to use the lawn in a couple of months.

Long-term lawn care

Once established, lawns still need regular attention – and not just from the lawn mower. It's very disheartening to put all that work into creating a well-prepared, level and weed-free lawn if the site deteriorates once it's in use.

ABOVE: A standard picnic table can be moved around the lawn, according to the season, to find the cosiest spot.

Mowing

Regular mowing is essential if you want to keep your lawn looking good. Try to mow once a week when the lawn is growing. This may seem arduous, but you'll find that the less there is to cut off, the less time it takes. For a neat, traditional lawn with fine grass and stripes to set off your borders, you'll need a cylinder mower or a wheeled rotary mower with a rear roller. For more on mowing, see page 114.

Every time you cut the lawn you should cut the edges with a pair of edging shears to give a really neat finish. Tatty edges let a garden down badly.

Feeding

Not many people think about feeding their lawn – the last thing they want to do is make it grow. But it's not that simple. If you feed your lawn in spring using a feed specially formulated for that time of year, the transformation will amaze you. You'll suddenly realize that it wasn't green at all but a curious yellowish shade. The different brands vary in their staying power: some last all season, some just a few weeks, so you may need to treat the lawn more than once.

It's important not to use the spring feed too late in the season. Change to an autumn feed that stimulates root growth and sets the lawn up for the cold weather. For more on lawn feeds, see page 96.

Weeds and moss

Weeds in a small lawn are disfiguring but also easy to deal with. There are a number of products that combine spring and summer lawn feed with weedkiller, and treatments of this type are especially effective. The feed stimulates the grass to grow into the gaps left by the dead weeds. Lawn weedkillers are available in liquid or dry formulations but must be kept off plants in the beds and borders, as they'll kill these too. If you decide to use a liquid one, buy an extra watering can, label it and keep it just for weedkillers. After all, you don't want to risk watering weedkiller on to your geraniums.

If you prefer not to treat the whole lawn, rosette weeds like daisies and dandelions can be removed by cutting the roots with an old knife. There are also ozone-friendly aerosols that can be used to squirt a dab of foam containing a lawn weedkiller on to individual weeds – these make treating dandelions and daisies easy.

Moss can be more of a problem. It's not difficult to kill moss, but unless you deal with the reasons for its presence, it will keep coming back. Many lawn weedkillers also contain a moss killer, and specific moss killers are also available. These are very effective and kill moss quickly, while some brands also prevent moss growth for the rest of the season.

Moss growth is usually caused by shade or poor drainage, or both – these conditions are not only good for moss but bad for grass. In small gardens that are unavoidably shaded, the answer is usually to dig up the lawn. You can prepare for new lawns on badly drained sites by forking in grit. It's more difficult to deal with moss in an established lawn that you wish to keep and that is unavoidably shaded. Improving the drainage is usually the only help. Or you could take the contrary approach and encourage moss – it can look delightful, although it's not a good surface for games.

Drainage and aeration

It's a straightforward but arduous business to improve lawn drainage once the lawn is down; it's just as well we're limiting the discussion to small gardens. In autumn or spring, using a digging fork, make holes to about half the depth of the prongs all over the lawn; each set of holes should be about 15cm/6in apart. Then spread some sharp sand over the surface and work it into the holes, using a stiff broom or the back of a garden rake. Keep this up until the holes are full of sand. These drainage holes will help take the water away from the soil surface quickly.

Another way to discourage moss and keep the grass growing vigorously is to rake out all the dead stems (thatch). In old lawns you'll often find that the green shoots are actually growing on top of a 2.5cm/1in layer of thatch. You can use a wire rake but it's very hard work, so I recommend hiring an electric lawn raker, which will do a wonderful job (see page 92).

Beds and borders

This is what gardens are all about. It's very nice to have patios for barbecues and lawns to relax on, but it's the plants that really count. First of all, perhaps we ought to decide the difference between a bed and a border. Any planting area entirely surrounded by grass, paving or path is a bed. Any long, wide planting area backed by a wall, fence, hedge or path is a border. More or less...

Positioning your border

The positioning of beds and borders is fundamental to the design of the garden. Here are a few pointers.

- Be more cautious about making planting areas too small than too large.
- Try to ensure that all walls and fences have planting areas in front of them.
- Avoid long straight borders parallel to boundaries unless you can raise them (see page 146) or they're part of a consciously formal plan.
- Beds and borders in a mixture of formal and informal shapes can jar. Choose one or the other, or think carefully before mixing them.
- Don't make them all the same shape and size.

Planning your border

It's a good idea to think about what you are going to plant in your beds as you decide where to site them, and how big they're to be. If you like grey and silver foliage plants, think about making a special planting area in a sunny site. Do you prefer mixed borders with shrubs, climbers, perennials, bulbs and annuals, or do you take a more traditional approach and like to keep an area exclusively for hardy herbaceous perennials? Here are a few guidelines, but remember that they are there to be adapted to suit your own wishes.

- After two years there should be no bare soil visible.
- Foliage is just as important as flowers.

OPPOSITE: Make most of your planting a mixture of shrubs, climbers, perennials and bulbs, but devote at least one area to a narrower group.

- Don't be afraid to try something new, but if it isn't a success, abandon it.
- If something doesn't work, change it.
- Make the most of mixed planting, but make provision for at least one area devoted to a narrower group.
- Give most beds and borders themes. This not only gives them character, but also helps you to plan what you're going to plant. Examples of broad themes might be: spring flowers, winter colour, foliage plants, seasonal flowers, cottage garden plants, alpines. Examples of narrower themes might be: grey foliage, white flowers, primroses and snowdrops, old-fashioned roses.
- Don't be restricted by your soil. In a small garden, making raised beds for different planting mixtures is not difficult.
- Always make provision for temporary seasonal plantings of annuals and spring bedding in containers, in gaps in mixed borders or in beds of their own.

Planting design

Giving advice on planting is a risky business, because whatever recommendations an author makes there will always be people who disagree. However, here are some general points that no one is likely to disagree with.

The first point perhaps needs amplification. Dense planting implies a well-filled, mature-looking garden with lots to see and little space for the weeds to sneak through. Obviously it would be unrealistic to expect all your shrubs to reach maturity almost instantly, but the gaps between them can be filled with seasonals and easily propagated ground-cover plants whose allocation of space can be reduced as the more important plants spread. In fact it's important not to let annuals shade out the lower branches of young shrubs, because their shape may be ruined.

Tall plants should usually go at the back and shorter ones at the front, but don't stick rigidly to this rule; if you do, the result is likely to be predictable and dull.

In mixed borders you need shrubs to create a permanent framework to your planting. In many cases

these can be trained against walls and fences so that they don't take up too much space. It may be tempting to choose only evergreens, but this can be dull; mix them with deciduous types for more variety.

Never be afraid to mix things. For example, if you intermingle daffodils and hostas, the attractive hosta foliage not only follows the daffodil flowers but also hides their dying foliage. And you can plant climbers like clematis under shrubs to scramble up through them.

Preparation

Once you've marked out the area of your bed or border, it should be dug over and plenty of organic matter worked in (see page 99). This is the time to prepare soil for different types of plants. So if you want to grow woodland plants on a gravelly soil, fork in even more organic matter than you would use normally, and if necessary raise the level of the beds a little using rocks, old bricks, timber or half-poles (split logs stapled to a wire backing, also known as logroll). If you plan a

Mediterranean bed and your soil is heavy, this is the time to add grit to improve the drainage in winter.

It's vital that the roots of perennial weeds are removed at this stage, and there's a good argument for growing mostly seasonals in the first year. If a mass of bindweed comes up among the petunias, it's not serious if you have to dig them out to get at the bindweed roots – they would only last one season anyway; moving your newly planted magnolia is another matter.

Planting

Although the books all say 'plant the shrubs first', the fact is that we all buy plants when we happen upon something we like and they must then be found a home. Don't worry about it – just put them into

ABOVE: Neat foliage plants with harmonizing colours and contrasting shapes make an attractive long-season planting.

OPPOSITE: A mixed border teeming with flowers and foliage gives the impression of a mature garden and leaves little room for weeds.

a suitable space and give them room to grow. Putting the shrubs in early is good advice, however, for not only do they take longer to mature, but it's easier to fit the smaller, more movable plants in around them rather than to find room to fit shrubs in among the perennials.

Take no notice of the old rules about only planting in the autumn, or the more modern suggestion to plant only in the spring. Now that most plants are available in containers, except sometimes fruit and those from specialist mail-order nurseries, we can buy them in flower, when we can see how they'll perform, and they can be planted at any time of year when the ground is suitable.

There is, though, the important proviso that, if you plant in summer, you must keep your plants well watered, and especially so in hot climates. This is especially important now that so many plants are sold in peat-only or peat-based composts. If these dry out after planting, it can be difficult to re-wet them again and the plants will suffer.

It's often convenient to accumulate the plants for a bed while it's being prepared and then put in all the permanent plants in one session. This is a very helpful approach if your planting is to have a particular theme. Planting in one burst also gives a great sense of achievement, and if the gaps are filled with annuals, the bed will be full in its first year.

In a small garden, where plants and paving, plants and timber, plants and fences, plants and furniture – in fact plants and everything else – jostle together closely, these combinations of colour and form can bring a mass of delightful detail to the garden. So where plants will be interacting visually with any other materials, choose their colour and form to make satisfying associations with the boards, paving or gravel alongside.

ABOVE RIGHT: Boards can be used to edge a mixed bed and keep the garden neat; lay them out on site first, with their supports, then set them in place and add a mulch.

RIGHT: This colour themed border is so full that weeds will never get a foothold, but the taller plants will need support.

OPPOSITE: The different habits of growth of these three perennials make a satisfying combination.

Chapter 3

The Practicalities

It's all very well having great ideas for planting schemes, but you won't get very far if you don't have the tools and technical knowledge to realize them. Even the smallest garden requires some basic equipment in order to prepare the area for planting as well as for regular maintenance work. Some of these tools are essential and therefore worth buying; others can be hired as necessary. To give your plants a good start, you also need to get your soil in the best condition you can, and once planted, basic tasks such as weeding and pruning should be carried out regularly.

Tools

Most of us find ourselves with a collection of garden tools made up of cast-offs or presents from relatives, plus oddments we found in the shed when we moved house. This is then augmented with what we buy, with a greater or lesser degree of inspiration, from the garden centre or DIY store. Sometimes this makes up an adequate collection, sometimes not.

Essentials

You don't need many garden tools. It's possible to get by with just a border fork and an old bread knife – possible, but not very convenient. However, don't make the mistake of rushing out to buy lots of expensive items as soon as you start gardening. You don't need a shedful of sparkling new tools to be a good gardener; instead, start by borrowing from friends and neighbours, looking for second-hand tools at car boot sales and flea markets, and buying the occasional new item. And keep your gift list up to date.

The basics include:
- spade;
- border fork;
- rake;
- hoe;
- secateurs (hand pruners);
- hand fork;
- watering equipment and hosepipe;
- gloves;
- lawn mower and edging shears (if you have a lawn).

Spade

A stainless steel spade will make preparing your soil a great deal easier. Soil doesn't stick to a stainless steel blade, so digging is less arduous; ordinary steel blades will need cleaning much more often, especially if your soil is heavy. A timber handle is warmer to the touch than a steel one. Compare models, prices and comfort in the garden centre or DIY store.

Border fork

One of the most useful of all tools, the border fork (even now sometimes still called a lady's fork!) is a smaller version of a digging fork. It's useful for a wide variety of gardening tasks, including loosening the soil surface and working in organic matter, preparing the ground for planting, handling organic matter and collecting debris.

Garden rake

A rake is essential for sowing seed, helping to prepare the soil in a new garden, making a lawn and simply producing a neat finish. It can also be used for

ABOVE: Sharp secateurs are one of the most essential of tools; try to handle them first to be sure they're comfortable and buy the best quality pair you can afford.
OPPOSITE: A small-bladed spade with a wooden handle is the ideal tool for planting up new beds and borders.

collecting leaves from the lawn. An alloy handle takes the hard work out of raking.

Hoe

There are many types of hoe, and it is an invaluable tool for keeping new borders and vegetable beds weed-free. The most widely used type is the Dutch hoe, with the handle attached to both sides of the blade, but I find this awkward when working close to plants. On other designs the handle joins the blade in the centre or on one side, allowing the blade to slide under the edges of plants without bruising them. These are excellent. Again, hoes with plastic-coated alloy handles are the lightest in weight and very easy to use.

Secateurs

A good pair of secateurs (hand pruners) is vital, and is used not only for pruning but also for taking cuttings. It's not always easy to handle secateurs in the shop, but

try to choose a pair that fits your hand; remember, though, that a small pair will not cut thick branches and you will need to use long-handled loppers for heavier work. Left-handed models are available.

Hand fork

A hand fork is extremely useful for removing small weeds, titivating the soil surface and, if you don't have a trowel, planting small plants. Avoid those with plastic handles, which will give you blisters after a few minutes' use; a fork with a wooden handle and stainless steel blade is the best option.

Trowel

Matching the hand fork in size, a stainless steel trowel will get plenty of use, not only in a new garden where there's regular planting to do but also in any garden where improvements are being made. If you're thinking of asking for a hand fork for a present, you might as well ask for a stainless steel trowel and hand fork set.

Sprinkler

Some form of watering is essential in any garden, but especially so when many new plants are going in or when mature specimens are being moved. A sprinkler is the simplest option, but don't forget that you may need a licence from your local water company to use it.

The design that combines the most even water distribution with adjustability and the ability to function well on low pressure is the type with a slowly oscillating curved bar punctured with holes to create a fan-shaped spray. Sometimes called lawn sprinklers, these water a more or less square or rectangular area, which is usually more convenient than a circular spray pattern.

Seephose/soakerhose

This is the responsible, and economic, way to water the garden. Seephose, also known as soakerhose and leaky pipe, is a black, flexible microperforated rubber pipe that

is laid among the plants and covered with mulch. Water seeps through the pores and drains direct into the soil with the minimum of wasteful evaporation.

Hosepipe

It's no good having a sprinkler or seephose if you have no hosepipe to connect it to the tap. Buy a length of laminated hosepipe reinforced with braided nylon, long enough to reach every corner of the garden with some to spare. Buy a hose reel to keep it stored neatly, and quick-locking hose fittings to connect the sprinkler. You can also use the hose for watering containers.

Watering can

A watering can is invaluable for watering in new plantings and is also useful for containers. Plastic is lighter than steel but may degrade if kept out in the sun. Look for a can that comes with, or has available, a rose (the round or oval sprinkly bit with lots of holes that goes on the spout) made of brass, which will produce a fine, even spray. A can that is wide and low is usually better balanced than one that is tall and narrow.

Gloves

Some gardeners refuse to go into the garden without their gloves; others refuse to use them and like to 'stay in touch with the soil'. Believe me, if you're clearing an overgrown garden you need gloves as protection against nettles and brambles. If you prefer to keep your fingers clean and protect your manicure, wear gloves. Otherwise it's good to feel the soil on your fingers. There's a wealth of garden glove types now available. Some people prefer stout leather gloves; if you find these too cumbersome, try the disposable surgical gloves that are available by the boxful in the supermarket. Pigskin garden gloves are made from a more supple sort of leather. There are also garden gloves in women's sizes, and even 'bionic' garden gloves designed by surgeons to lessen hand fatigue.

Lawn mower

Electric mowers are ideal for a small garden, but the controversy continues over the best style of small lawn

OPPOSITE: Whatever type of mower you choose, always use a grass box to reduce mess and to help prevent the spread of weeds.

mower. My experience is that hover mowers, even those with grass bags, scatter the grass where it's not wanted and is difficult to collect – over gravel paths, for example. It's better to choose a conventional cylinder mower with a roller at the back to give you stripes and a rear-mounted, rather than front-mounted, grass box that allows you to get close to walls, fences and plants. Or go for a rotary mower with four wheels at the corners, or with two at the front and a roller for stripes at the back. The grass box or bag will be rear-mounted.

Lawn edger

I've known people cut the lawn edges with kitchen scissors, but I can hardly recommend it. A pair of long-handled edging shears with vertically set blades is what you need – as distinct from grass shears with horizontally set blades for cutting the grass round trees and along fences. Lawn-edging machines are unnecessary in a small garden.

String

Polypropylene twine lasts longest but tends to come in bright, unpleasant colours that stand out too much. Tarred string lasts a long time but is smelly and the tar comes off on your fingers. Green or brown twine is discreet and lasts well enough. Indeed, for tying up climbers it helps if the string rots after a couple of years because this prevents it from cutting into the swelling stems. Baler twine tangles and splits.

Plant ties

An increasing range of plant ties is available, often on a roll from which you can snip the length you need. Plastic-coated wire ties can be very useful and last longer than twine, but may last too well and bite into expanding stems.

Canes and stakes

Bamboo canes are becoming increasingly expensive but are still the most suitable for many jobs. If you think you'll need long ones for beans and sweet peas and also shorter ones for perennials, buy a stock of 2.4m/8ft

canes and cut some in half; one 2.4m/8ft cane is generally cheaper than two 1.2m/4ft canes. For large and weighty plants like dahlias, 25 x 25mm/1 x 1in stakes are more useful. Paint them with preservative if they're not already treated, and repeat the treatment when you pull them out and clean them in the autumn. In winter, store canes and stakes in a dry place, laid flat.

Netting

There are many types of plastic netting, with different uses. Wide mesh netting, about 15 x 10cm/6 x 4in, is used to keep pigeons and crows off vegetables and fruit and also as a support for peas, beans, sweet peas and other annual climbing plants. Small mesh netting, about 2.5 x 2.5cm/1 x 1in, is used to keep small birds like sparrows and finches off fruit and vegetables.

Heavy-duty netting with a 5 x 5cm/2 x 2in mesh is fixed to walls and fences to support perennial climbers like clematis, and is also used to form compost and leaf heaps. Heavy but very fine-meshed netting is used as greenhouse shading, and there are also special grades for use as windbreaks.

Garden chemicals

When I first became interested in organic gardening I was regarded as a crank; now gardening without chemicals is normal. In short, organic gardening involves not using artificial fertilizers or other garden chemicals. Instead, the soil is fed with bulky organic matter, and the plants with organic fertilizers derived from plants and animals. Natural predators and parasites are encouraged to help deal with pest problems, along with carefully considered cultural methods and natural insecticides when such treatments are necessary. A great deal of the success of organic gardening, though, is due to encouraging a balance of nature so that pests never get out of control, and growing the plants well so that they ride out any attacks from which they may suffer.

OPPOSITE: A simple bamboo cane and a string tie make the simplest and most effective support for both new and established plants.

However, some gardeners are still happy to use chemicals when necessary, taking the appropriate safety precautions. Others prefer only organic preparations, and others refuse to use any at all. I would say only that, especially in a small garden that is likely to be densely planted, you will be very lucky to avoid using chemicals altogether and still have healthy plants.

Pre-mixed ready-to-use sprays are the most convenient and the safest to use; products change almost every year but each is required to make it clear on the pack exactly what you can expect it to do. All are rigorously tested and approved by government agencies and they work well, and are certified as safe, provided you follow the instructions carefully.

Remember that chemicals can be dangerous, so treat them with respect from the moment you look at them in the garden centre. Store both organic and inorganic products where children cannot reach them.

Read the information on the pack before you buy, to ensure that the product will do what you want it to do and that it's suitable for the plants you wish to treat. Do not mix different products together to treat two different problems; look instead for the products with a wide range of applications or that deal with all the common problems of a specific plant.

Useful, but not essential

You may find a shovel, digging fork, long-handled loppers, hedging shears, hand cultivator and hoe, bucket, sprayer and bulb planter useful.

What you can borrow or hire

There are some tools that you will need occasionally but not often enough to make them worth buying. Some you can hire; others you can share with a friend or neighbour.

Wheelbarrow

You'll rarely need a wheelbarrow in a small garden, so borrow one when you do. If you find you use it

ABOVE: Wire or plastic netting is the best means of protecting new seedlings, particularly of fruit and vegetables, from birds.

OPPOSITE: An old timber wheelbarrow may be a little heavier to move around but looks for more attractive than a plastic or steel model.

regularly and decide to buy one, don't buy a flimsy little galvanized garden barrow. Buy a large barrow with a spherical front wheel that is lightweight, easy to push and is not made of steel so won't rust. Alternatively choose a builders' barrow that is tough and has pneumatic tyres.

Wire rake

A wire rake is useful for removing thatch from the smallest lawns, but an electric lawn raker is far more satisfactory. A wire rake can also be used to collect leaves and other debris, but is not usually an essential item. Borrow one when you need it. If you have areas of gravel in your garden, though, you will find a wire rake really useful.

Lawn raker

An electric lawn raker is an incredible machine for removing moss and dead stems from the lawn and generally revitalizing it. You use it only once a year, so hire one when you need it.

Strimmer and brushwood cutter

In overgrown gardens, a strimmer or brushwood cutter will make quick work of cutting down weeds or brambles in a fraction of the time it would take with a scythe or shears. A strimmer, or string trimmer, usually electrically powered, has a rotating nylon line at ground level that cuts through weeds very efficiently. Take care as the nylon can damage tree bark. The more powerful brushwood cutter, for brambles and other tough materials, is usually petrol-powered with a rotating steel blade. Brushwood cutters can be very dangerous but are very effective.

Both of these tools are available at hire shops. Always read the safety guide that comes with these machines, wear protective goggles and stout boots when using them, and keep children safely indoors.

ABOVE: Use a simple garden line to mark out raised beds for vegetables, adjusting the layout until it's just right.

OPPOSITE: When rejuvenating an overgrown hedge, always use a pruning saw or long-handled loppers rather than secateurs for a neat finish.

Chain saw

If you have trees to remove, hire a chain saw. It is essential that you follow strict safety procedures when using this type of machinery. If you have the slightest qualms, or for anything taller than about 3.6m/12ft, hire an expert to carry out the removal for you. In a small garden it's so easy to smash a fence, a window or even yourself when a branch or the whole tree falls the wrong way or topples you off your ladder. And remember that for the cost of hiring a chain saw for a day, you can probably buy a large bow saw that will last for years and is much safer.

Hedge trimmer

Electric hedge trimmers are light in weight, and models with cutting edges on both sides of the bar are easiest to use. Even if your hedge is a short one, it's still worth hiring or buying a trimmer, and don't forget that hedges need trimming only once or twice a year. Small rechargeable battery-operated trimmers are often compatible with drills and other devices from the same manufacturer.

Pruning saw

A pruning saw is used mainly for those larger pruning jobs that are beyond secateurs or long-handled loppers, so obviously will be redundant in a new garden in which there are no trees or shrubs on which to use it. In an established garden there may be a need for a pruning saw, although your long-handled loppers will cope with most jobs.

What you can make

Some things you don't need to borrow and don't need to buy – you can make them.

Garden line

A garden line is exactly what its name implies – a piece of string that you use for guidance whenever you need a straight line. Take some stout sisal string or polypropylene twine, tie one end securely to a 45cm/18in piece of scrap timber, wind on more than you think you'll need, and tie the other end to another piece of timber. End of story. Do not use baler twine, which kinks and twists.

Measuring stick

This is one of the most useful of all garden tools, and simplicity itself to make. Take a 2m/7ft piece of 50 x 25mm/2 x 1in timber and make a saw cut across one side every 200mm and across the other side every 6in. Add extra cuts every 25mm and every 1in for the first 200mm and 12in, to give smaller measurements over a short length. Then give the whole thing two coats of green outdoor timber preservative. When it's dry, mark every major division (200mm and 12in) with two red-headed drawing pins, and every 100mm and 6in division with one pin so that you can see the marks at a glance.

Use your measuring stick when planting out, sowing seeds and as a guide when drawing drills. The only danger is that you'll tread on it and snap it in two.

Storage

Tools need storing in a dry place and the shed is the obvious spot, but there are alternatives (see page 41).

Inside you can either fit a purpose-made tool rack or simply use 15cm/6in nails, knocked in pre-drilled holes to avoid splitting the timber, with a pair of nails for each tool with a D- or T-handle; the rake and hoe go in the roof space, laid on the cross supports. Nails can also be placed to take shears. Trowel and hand fork usually live in an empty bucket. Secateurs are better kept in the house, where it's warm and dry and rust is less likely to attack the cutting edge.

Hosepipe should not be left lying on the ground filled with water, especially in frosty weather. Keep it on a hose reel, or coil it evenly on the floor in the shed. Never hang it on a nail, because it will corrode where the nail kinks it.

Electrical equipment – lawn mowers, for example – must be stored in the dry, so check existing garden sheds to ensure that they really are waterproof.

Maintenance

All tools should always be wiped clean of loose dirt after use – that, at least, many of us can manage. Then, every so often, wash spades and forks down, dry them off and spray them with an oil aerosol. Cutting tools need the same treatment. Secateurs that have become encrusted with plant sap can be cleaned by soaking them overnight in a solution of vinegar or biological washing powder, and this is even more successful if they're dismantled first. Never leave tools lying outside in the garden when you've finished using them – they'll sooner or later deteriorate and you'll have to go to the expense and bother of replacing them.

Mowers should be brushed off after each use, and grass that has collected under the hood and on or around the blades should be scraped off. Inspect the cable regularly for damage, but do not attempt to repair cuts and abrasions with tape; either shorten the cable by removing the section from the point of damage to the nearest end, or replace the cable entirely.

OPPOSITE: Crowded borders and intermingling climbers, like this clematis and perennial sweet pea, in a small garden will need regular applications of fertilizer to keep them thriving and the soil nourished.

Soil improvers and fertilizers

Garden centre shelves are sagging under the weight of far too many items that you may be tempted to buy. A few are vital, some are useful, most are a waste of money.

Dry fertilizers

Fertilizers are essential in one form or another. Although they do little lasting good to the soil, they're of great short-term benefit to plants. Many different types are available, often specially formulated to suit particular plants – tomatoes, roses, vegetables, etc.

Forget most of these for now, and buy the biggest bag you can afford of just one balanced general fertilizer. Store it in a dry place with the bag re-tied to keep out moisture. Apply it at around 60g (about a full handful) per square metre (2oz per square yard) every spring to all cultivated areas and rake it in. It can also be used in a planting mix made up of one bucketful of garden compost or used potting compost to two handfuls of fertilizer, forked into the planting holes before you set new plants in place.

Special fertilizers for specific plants can wait until the garden is established, or you can use liquid feeds. Always wear rubber gloves or disposable surgical gloves when handling fertilizers.

Liquid feeds

Liquid feeds are absorbed by the plant more quickly than dry fertilizers, so they give a quick tonic, help revive sickly specimens or provide a special balance of plant foods suitable for one particular crop. If you grow tomatoes, for instance, using a special tomato feed will greatly increase your crop.

Liquid feeds are available for tomatoes, cucumbers, roses, clematis, flowering pot plants, foliage pot plants, orchids, African violets and so on. There are also general liquid feeds suitable for a wide variety of crops. Tomato feed is the best all-rounder for flowering and fruiting plants and works especially well on summer containers. Do not buy a feed for every different type of plant you have; you'll end up with partly used bottles cluttering the shed shelf for years.

Lawn treatments

At its simplest a lawn treatment feeds the grass, and you'll be astonished how quickly one or two treatments can transform a yellowing lawn into a lush green carpet. Some treatments also include a moss killer, which is very useful if moss is a problem; others include a weedkiller. By using a combined weedkiller and lawn feed, the spaces left by the dead weeds are soon filled by the newly stimulated grass.

There are both liquid and dry lawn treatments available. Dry materials are easier to apply because their bright colour, which soon disappears, makes it obvious which areas of the lawn have been treated. But they need to be washed into the soil by rain before the lawn can be used so, if you have pets or young children, I would suggest using a liquid treatment instead. Once the liquid has dried on the grass, pets and children can use the lawn. Some treatments are intended for spring use, others for autumn, and it's important to use the right one.

Lime

Your soil test kit (see page 19) will tell you the pH (alkalinity/acidity) of your soil and advise you whether you need to apply lime and, if so, how much to apply. Always wear protective gloves when handling lime.

Organic matter

Organic matter is one of the most important materials to the gardener – indeed, it's almost a universal panacea. It improves just about any soil, and is especially useful in new and neglected gardens. It breaks up clay soils, binds together sandy soils, makes soil more workable and even prevents weed growth when spread on the surface. It holds a reservoir of water, while at the same time encouraging surplus moisture to drain away. As it rots it releases nutrients that are taken up by the plants. Organic matter comes in many forms, and needs to be constantly replaced.

Garden compost

Weeds and vegetable refuse can be made into valuable compost in the garden (see page 112). This will often contain weed seeds, so is best dug into the soil and not spread on the surface where the weeds will soon grow.

Lawn mowings

These are a poor source of organic matter. Never spread grass cuttings directly on your beds and borders, as they almost always contain grass seeds that will soon produce a forest of weeds. Compost them, using a compost activator specifically for lawn mowings to help them rot down.

Autumn leaves

Leaves are an excellent source of organic matter but are best stacked on their own without weeds or other vegetable waste. They can take two years to rot down. In some areas, local authorities may collect fallen leaves from parks and streets, and composted leaves may be available for the asking.

Peat

Peat is no longer considered appropriate as a soil improver. The destruction of peat bogs in England, Ireland, Russia, Finland and Scandinavia, Canada, the United States and elsewhere has led to justifiable campaigns against the use of bulk peat to improve soils, and many alternatives are now available.

Peat alternatives

A number of organic soil improvers are now available. These may comprise bark and wood waste, paper waste, coconut fibre (coir), fruit fibre, sewage sludge, chicken or animal manure and various other organic materials. They are generally clean and easy to handle, with no distasteful smells, and are excellent soil improvers.

Bark

This comes in two forms – chipped and composted. Chips are used as a mulch on the surface to retain moisture, suppress weeds and produce a neat finish; composted bark is also used as a mulch, especially on small beds, but also to improve the soil before planting.

Manure

Well-rotted horse or farmyard manure is the richest form of organic matter, but is messy, can be smelly and is not easy to come by unless you live in or near the country. Stable manure may be advertised at the roadside, or in the local paper, sometimes free; always

ABOVE: A mulch of bark chips helps prevent weed growth, retains moisture in the soil and sets off the plants well.

OPPOSITE: Dandelions are often a feature of neglected lawns but can be cut out with an old knife or treated with weedkiller.

take it from the bottom of the stack where it will be well rotted. Never load it into the car in bin bags – the bags will burst (followed by your temper); use empty fertilizer sacks or other stout bags and never overfill them. Never put raw, fresh manure on the garden; it must rot down first. Well-rotted manure in sealed bags, together with a range of other bulky organic products, is becoming widely available in garden centres.

Clay cures

You will find products on sale described as clay breakers or clay cures. These are not cheap: don't buy them. Instead, spend the money on bulky organic matter that will do the same job, probably better, while also improving the soil in other ways.

Techniques

Even the absolute beginner can succeed in growing healthy plants, partly because the basic gardening skills are not difficult to pick up, but also because plants are amazingly resilient – they have an unfailing urge to grow, and it's hard to stop them.

Digging

There are two types of digging – single digging and double digging. They differ in the depth to which the soil is dug. Double digging, to a depth of 45cm/18in or more, is, frankly, too much like hard work. You will grow better plants if you dig deep, but if you think about how much time and energy you'll have to spend before you plant anything, you'll probably not bother.

So, single digging it is – digging to the depth of your spade. Before you even start to dig, fork over part of the plot and look for the roots of nasty perennial weeds. These are usually easy to recognize, as they will probably be slender and carrot-like or white and wiry. At this stage you may well want to destroy them, perhaps with a systemic weedkiller, before you start digging. Dealing with these weeds now will certainly save you time and effort in the long run.

Single digging involves turning over and breaking up the top spit (the depth of your spade) of soil, about 25cm/10in. The purpose is to loosen the soil and make it more suitable for planting, and at the same time to improve the soil by adding organic matter.

ABOVE: Forking over the soil allows weeds and large stones to be removed and also improves the appearance of beds and borders.

The area to be dug should be cleared of debris, and any plants you wish to keep should be removed before you start digging. Next, divide the plot in half, using your garden line to create two rectangles. Start at the narrow end of one rectangle. Mark out an area 30cm/12in long, using your measuring stick (see page 93), and if the plot is still a little weedy, slice off the top 2.5cm/1in of soil together with the weeds and stack it on a sheet of polythene alongside the end of the other rectangle, at the same end of the plot.

Now, using your digging spade, dig out all the soil from the measured area to the depth of your spade and stack this on the sheet of polythene too. If you've not used a weedkiller and you have perennial weeds, their roots will now be revealed and should be removed and kept separate from other weeds for burning or dumping later. This is the point at which the organic matter is added. Simply spread it in the bottom of the trench to a depth of 5–7.5cm/2–3in.

The next step is to slice off any annual weeds from the next 30cm/12in of soil and lay them in the trench on top of the organic matter. Now work backwards down the plot, excavating the next 30cm/12in of soil and using it to fill the trench in front of you, covering the organic matter and the weeds. You should then be left with 30cm/12in of soil rather higher than the rest of the plot, followed by a new trench. The organic matter goes in the new trench and so on down the plot until you get to the end.

Here you will end up with an empty 30cm/12in trench with nowhere to go next – except back down the other side of the plot in the opposite direction. So the weeds and soil from the strip alongside your empty trench are turned in, and you then work in exactly the same way back up the other side of the plot to where you started. When you arrive alongside the point where you started, you'll find a pile of soil and weeds from the very first trench; these are used to fill the last trench. You can then go and have a shower, pour yourself a well-deserved glass of wine and swear never to lift a spade again.

The hardest thing when you're learning to dig a plot is to leave a level surface, and this is especially difficult if the plot is uneven in width. Use a rake to level it out.

With double digging, you fork the organic matter into the bottom of the trench so that, in all, you loosen about 50cm/20in of soil. This is often easier to manage if you work with trenches 60cm/2ft wide.

Digging hints and tips

Digging seems a singularly laborious business, and it is; but it's worth it. Here are a few more guidelines.
- Eliminate all perennial weeds, either by weedkilling before you start or by carefully removing the roots as you go.
- Ideally, heavy clay soil is best dug in the autumn and early winter, as the frost helps break down the clods. Lighter, sandy soil can be left until early spring.
- If you are not used to digging, do just a little at a time. It's far better to do half an hour every evening after work and two half-hours each day at the weekend than attempt to do the whole lot in one weekend; you will injure your back.
- Do not dig when the soil is frozen, waterlogged or bone dry.

Incorporating organic matter

Digging provides an opportunity to incorporate organic matter into the soil and this can be done in one of two ways: the easy way and the best way.

The easy way is to put a layer 5–7.5cm/2–3in deep in the bottom of each trench as you work down the plot, covering it with soil as you go, as described above. This, of course, leaves all the organic matter in a single layer and it's not until the worms have got to work, or the next time you dig, that it's mixed in more evenly. It's far better to mix the organic matter into the soil.

If the soil has been dug relatively recently and is not infested with weeds, then rather than digging the plot with a spade you can spread organic matter on the surface and work it in with a digging fork. Otherwise, spread it on the surface after digging and work it into

the loose soil with a fork. The organic matter needs to be fine and friable and not lumpy if you are forking it in, so garden compost must be well rotted. Alternatively, use a bought soil improver.

This sounds like hard work, but it's obvious that organic matter spread more or less evenly through the depth of the soil will be of more benefit to plant roots than if it sits in a single layer 23cm/9in deep.

Rotary cultivation

The alternative to digging – and my preference as I already have a bad back – is to hire a rotary cultivator. These are invaluable machines that loosen the soil and blend in organic matter very effectively, but they have certain disadvantages: few of the models available for hire will deal with compacted soil and they can be difficult to handle if you're not fit.

Rotary cultivators are not cheap to hire, and you may even find that if your garden is a very small one, it's more economical to pay someone to dig it than to hire a machine for a day. Always try to hire a model with powered drive wheels as well as powered tines, as it will be easier to manoeuvre and more likely to do a good job.

In soil conditions where they function well, rotary cultivators leave the soil fine and easily worked; it's a treat to plant in it. The soil will need a few weeks to settle before planting, or you could tread it down. If you spread your organic matter on the surface of the plot after you have been over it once and then go over it again with the cultivator, it should mix thoroughly in with the soil.

Forking

Areas that are in reasonably good heart benefit from being forked over with a border fork between plantings. For example, when replacing a clump of worn-out perennials the soil should be forked over before new

OPPOSITE: As well as using your rake to create a fine finish on newly prepared areas, the back of the rake can be used to firm the soil gently over newly sown seeds.

plants are put in. The soil is simply turned over without bothering to make a trench, and broken down by hitting it with the back of the fork. Friable organic matter is worked in at the same time. Light forking between plants to perhaps half the depth of the tines, or even less, leaves an attractive surface finish.

Treading

It may seem strange, having conscientiously loosened the soil by digging, to firm it again, but if left loose, not only will it sink after you've set your plants, but the water will also drain through too quickly. In addition, the increased amount of air in the soil will encourage it to dry out.

Soil should be trodden in an organized way – it's no good just wandering over it aimlessly while listening to your personal stereo. Start in one corner and then shuffle along the edge, leaving a row of heel prints in a side-by-side pattern. Then move across, turn round and make another row alongside the first until the plot is covered. This is an exhausting business, so do it in two or three stages rather than in one session if you need to.

Raking

After digging, levelling roughly and treading, you'll need to rake the soil level to leave a good finish before planting or sowing seeds. The secret of effective raking is to move the rake in long flowing strides and not in short stabs. You may find it easier to bend over to achieve this, as there's a tendency to work more jerkily when standing upright. Try not to remove too many stones or you'll find the whole business never-ending – and you'll have a vast heap of debris requiring disposal.

For beds and borders the soil level does not have to be perfect, especially as it will be altered by the soil you remove when digging out planting holes. For a lawn it's more important, and it pays to rake level as best you can after treading and then leave it until after a heavy downpour. Then, when the soil has dried out a little, rake it again. If you're adding fertilizer, do so after the final raking and then rake again lightly.

Planting

Plants are available in different forms and require different planting techniques.

Container-grown shrubs

Ornamental shrubs and some fruit bushes are most commonly sold growing in containers, usually semi-rigid black pots. They can be planted at any time when the ground is not bone dry, waterlogged or frozen, but spring and autumn are the best times. Water the plant well, adding liquid feed to the water, the day before you plant.

Having decided where your shrub or fruit bush is to be planted, dig out a hole twice as wide as the pot and the same depth as the blade of your spade. Pile the soil around the hole. Fork over the bottom of the hole loosely, then work in a bucketful of organic matter – garden compost is ideal or, alternatively, use a bought soil improver. Firm it with the toe of your boot. Then mix some more compost into some of the soil from the hole that you've piled round the edge.

Now stand the plant in the hole, still in its container. Lay a bamboo cane across the hole, or simply look carefully, and add or remove soil until the top of the compost in the container is about 2.5cm/1in below the cane. Make sure that the best side of the shrub is facing in the direction from which it will usually be viewed. Remove the plant from the pot by grasping it around its base and tapping the rim of the pot with a trowel, then place the plant in the hole. Do not disturb the roots. Refill the hole around the roots with the soil-and-compost mix until it's just above the surface of the plant's compost; firm with your fingers or, for large shrubs, your toes, as you go. A slight depression should be left to collect water.

Water the plant well, again adding a liquid feed to the water, then mulch with 5cm/2in of weed-free mulch.

Shrubs and fruit bushes rarely need staking, but conifers and other evergreens in exposed positions benefit from a windbreak. This can consist simply of plastic windbreak netting nailed to three stakes in a V, pointing into the prevailing wind.

Bare-root and root-balled shrubs

Usually only fruit bushes, and sometimes hedging plants, are sold bare-root; they're grown in the ground at the nursery, dug from the soil, the soil is shaken off their roots and they're sold with their roots bare and usually packed carefully in a plastic bag. Sometimes the soil is retained and the roots are wrapped in sacking and secured with string or wire (root-balled). In some areas shrubs and trees are also sold in this way. Late autumn or early spring is the best time to plant bare-root and root-balled bushes, although any time before they start to grow in spring is acceptable.

Soak bare roots overnight in water, with liquid feed added to help give them a flying start, then prepare the hole in the same way as for container-grown shrubs. Try to leave a 15cm/6in space around the roots. However, the guide for the final level will not be the surface of the compost in the container but the old planting level, usually the top of the wet-stained portion at the base of the stem. When refilling the hole, jiggle the roots slightly to ensure that soil filters around them and that no air spaces are left. Then firm with the fingers or toes.

Container-grown trees

Planting is exactly the same as for shrubs, though naturally the hole will be larger. The tree will also need staking; use two 90cm/3ft stakes, knocked in on either side of the root ball, plus a cross-piece nailed between them and a tree tie fixed to the tree about 30cm/12in above the ground. Choose a purpose-made tree tie that can be loosened as the trunk expands. Finally, water well with liquid feed and keep watering frequently until the tree is established.

Evergreen trees in windy positions need a windbreak consisting of plastic windbreak netting nailed to three stout stakes set in a V formation, and pointing into the direction of the wind.

OPPOSITE: Treat the plant and the container as a single feature and ensure that the two are in harmony in both colour and shape. This cobalt blue pot complements the brilliant foliage of the maple it contains.

Bare-root trees

Many fruit trees, and some ornamental trees, are sold
bare root. Late autumn is again the best time to plant.
The hole for bare-root trees is prepared in the same
way as that for container-grown shrubs, but leaving
a 23cm/9in space around the roots. The guide for the
final level is again the top of the wet-stained portion
at the base of the stem.

The tree should be orientated in its hole so that a gap
in the roots through which a stake can pass is on the
windward side. The tree can then be removed from the
hole and a 90cm/3ft stake can be knocked in, leaving
30–38cm/12–15in of the stake above the final soil level.
The tree can then be replaced and the hole refilled.
When refilling the hole, jiggle the roots slightly to
ensure that soil filters around them and that no air
spaces are left, then firm well. Finally, use a tree tie
to secure the tree to its stake, making sure that it is
not tied too tightly.

Small plants

Small plants such as shrubs and climbers in small
pots, small hardy perennials, rock plants, container and
seasonal plants, and vegetables are put in with a trowel,
taking out a hole just a little wider than the root ball
and sufficiently deep to leave the crown of the plant
at soil level. A little soil improver or planting mix is
worked into the hole with the trowel, then the plant
is set in place and the soil is replaced and firmed
with the fingers.

Bulbs

Bulbs are planted in beds and borders with a spade or
trowel. Plant them in clumps or irregular drifts and
never in rows, except in spring bedding schemes. Always
plant at the recommended depth: err on the deep side if
in doubt, especially in colder climates. Ensure that the
base of the hole is flat and that there's no gap under the
bulb where water can collect. On heavy soils a handful
of grit under the bulb helps prevent rotting; make the
initial hole slightly deeper. When planting bulbs in grass,
a bulb planter is very useful; again, plant in drifts or
clumps and never in rows.

Staking

Many plants – trees, perennials and annuals – need
support to protect them from wind, rain, snow and the

weight of their own flowers. Trees need support from a stout stake in their early years (see page 102). Perennials and annuals can be supported using a number of different materials: brushwood and canes are the traditional choices. Brushwood (especially the traditional hazel twigs) is now difficult to buy, not easy to store and is short-lived, but it is still the most effective method and the least visible when in use. Brushwood is sometimes available from local conservation groups.

Bamboo canes are altogether easier to use: one cane for two or three single stems of a border perennial, three around the outside for a large plant, five or seven around a group. Although it may be easier to push in the narrow end, canes will be more secure if the fat end goes in first. Where just one cane is used, single ties at different levels can be used to support up to three stems. For a group of plants, run string around the outside and cross it and loop it between the canes to support both the outside and the insides of the group.

Steel and plastic-covered frames are also available for supporting border plants; these are effective but expensive. Set them in a ring around the outside of the plant. The more sophisticated versions have a mesh of crossing wires through which the stems can grow.

Climbing plants like runner beans and sweet peas need tall supports. The simplest system is a wigwam-like structure made of a ring of 2.4m/8ft canes that are pushed into the ground by about 60cm/2ft, with the tops tied together with twine or locked with a plastic cane holder.

If you're growing more than just a few plants, a pair of stout stakes with a wire tensed between them at top and bottom to support wide-meshed plastic netting is ideal.

RIGHT: All trees should be supported with a short stake and plastic tree tie; be sure to loosen the tie as the trunk expands over the years.

OPPOSITE, ABOVE: Small bulbs like these crocus and hardy cyclamen will grow happily under deciduous shrubs and intermingle with dwarf perennials.

OPPOSITE, BELOW: Twiggy brushwood is often the most effective and unobtrusive way to support perennials like these heleniums. It can be difficult to find but is always worth hunting out.

Deadheading

Almost all flowering plants will be more productive if the dying flowers are picked off as they fade. Don't bother to deadhead very small-flowered plants like alyssum and lobelia – life's too short – although they can be clipped over quickly with hand shears and then watered if a dry spell follows. Shrubs that produce large numbers of small flowers are also impracticable to deadhead.

Larger flowers are easy to deadhead and are managed in different ways:
- Geranium flowers can be snapped off where they join the stem.
- Roses must be cut just a few leaves below the flower.
- Dahlias should be cut above the next flowering shoot lower down.
- Rhododendrons should have each dead flower snapped off on its short stalk.
- The dying flowers of most other plants are simply cut off above the next bud down.

Training shrubs

Most shrubs need little training. They're often pruned back by about one-third after planting to encourage bushy growth from low down on the plant, but otherwise, apart from any necessary regular pruning, they're simply left to get on with it.

Shrubs trained on walls and fences need more care. Both walls and fences should be wired to assist training (see page 54), which at its simplest will consist in choosing a number of major shoots and training them evenly into a fan shape to cover the space. Bamboo canes can be fixed to the wires to make the rays of the fan, as support for the main branches. One cane should be more or less upright, with the others roughly in matching pairs on either side.

When planting against a fence, the shrub should be orientated so that the maximum number of shoots are close to the wall for tying in. After planting the shrub, the canes can be slid into position and tied in and the shoots can be tied to them. Smaller side shoots not tied to canes can be tied to the wires. Any vigorous shoots growing out into the border should be cut back by half.

Training climbers

Much the same procedure outlined for shrubs applies for climbers, although their shoots are often more unruly and difficult to organize. You may find it easier to fix trellis to your fence or wall.

Mulching

Mulching is a method of applying organic matter to borders simply by spreading it over the surface of the soil between the plants. The mulch helps to conserve moisture in the soil, suppresses the growth of weeds, improves the soil quality and provides plant foods. It's essential that weed-free materials be used, such as composted bark or bark chips or one of the various peat substitutes. A depth of about 5–7.5cm/2–3in is usually about right; never mound the mulch against the trunks of trees or allow it to smother delicate young shoots.

Apply organic mulches in spring, when the soil is moist, or (preferably) in autumn after tidying the borders and weeding thoroughly.

ABOVE: A wide range of gravels and pebbles is now available for paths and for mulching; choose the colour, shape and size carefully.

OPPOSITE: Shrubs and climbers can be trained on a wall using a system of wires, a fan of canes or by tying stems to individual nails.

Raised beds, rock gardens and Mediterranean plantings, where plants require good drainage, should be mulched with grit or fine gravel at about 5cm/2in deep. Larger stones and small boulders make dramatic mulches among plants with a striking habit, like grasses.

An increasing range of mulches is now available, including coloured bark and coloured wood chips, rounded recycled coloured glass chips and steel waste.

Hoeing

Hoeing to kill weeds is ideal for crops that are grown in rows, like vegetables, and for new plantings where there's plenty of space between plants. In established borders the ground should be more or less covered in vegetation.

Use a sharp hoe, sharpening it with a coarse file if necessary. Keep the blade horizontal and move it back and forth just under the soil surface; do not dig it into the ground at an angle. Weeds will not need collecting unless they're about to drop their seeds or still have their

of clumps of perennial plants. They cannot be safely hoed off, so need to be removed by hand – they can often simply be pulled out, perhaps with the help of a hand fork.

Preventing weeds

Weeds are always with us, but a great deal of weed growth can be prevented.
• Never let weeds produce seed.
• Always clear the ground of all weeds, but especially perennial types, before planting.
• Apply a weed-suppressing mulch to borders in spring and/or autumn.
• For information on weed-suppressing plants, see page 234.

Watering

In hot climates, and as cool climates become drier, both ornamental and food plants need watering more. Enriching the soil with organic matter helps retain moisture, but there will always be times when you need to water – often regularly.

Don't worry too much about watering as soon as there's a week without rain, although for vegetables and fruit the situation can be more critical as so much of their bulk is made up of water. The problem arises if you apply a modest amount of water when there are still reserves deeper in the soil. For instead of questing down for moisture, roots will come to the surface, attracted by the small amount you've applied, which will not have sunk in very far. As the surface is the quickest area to dry out, the plants will then be more likely to suffer than if you had put no water on at all.

So when you water, leave the sprinkler on for an hour and a half so that the water sinks in well. Don't forget that you may need a licence to use a sprinkler, or indeed any hose attachment.

More effective, more economical and less troublesome is to use seephose/soakerhose to water your plants. This porous black pipe, usually made of recycled rubber, is laid on the beds in parallel rows and covered with mulch. On sandy soils the lengths are set closer than

roots attached; if it rains, weeds with roots still attached may well re-root.

Hoe when the soil surface is dry and the weather is sunny; weeds will soon shrivel and die. You will also find it much less time-consuming in the long run to hoe every week or two even if very few weeds are apparent.

Hand weeding

Weeds often grow close to other plants – among seedlings, in rows of vegetables, within groups of bulbs, around and among rock plants and in the middle on heavy clay soils. The seephose is connected by a length of conventional hose to an outside tap, and flow can be controlled by a timer or simply turned on when required. There may be no obvious sign that watering is taking place.

Spraying

The first thing to remember when it comes to spraying is that, whatever material you're using, you need to take precautions. Even organic materials can be irritating, or even poisonous, if treated carelessly.

Safety advice

The safety advice outlined here should be followed assiduously, whatever compound you are spraying.

- Always, and I mean always, read the instructions on the pack before starting to spray.
- Follow those instructions carefully – don't think that you know better than the manufacturer.
- Never skimp on any safety equipment or safety precautions recommended.
- Use granular materials and ready-to-use sprays whenever possible; do not use concentrates.
- Spray in calm conditions, preferably in the evening but not in hot sunshine.
- Do not spray plants in the conservatory if you can avoid it. Take the plants outside and then bring them back when the material has dried on the leaves.
- Never mix different chemicals together.
- Do not inhale vapours when spraying. A surgical mask is useful protection.
- Ensure that as much skin as possible is covered when spraying – don't wear shorts, roll down your sleeves and wear gloves.
- Keep pets and children away while you are spraying and until the spray has dried.

RIGHT: It's important to water in newly planted shrubs and climbers immediately after planting and to keep them moist during any dry spells afterwards.

OPPOSITE: This innovative little garden, mulched with recycled glass beads, will need any weeds removing by hand.

- Ensure that the whole plant is covered in spray, including as much of the underside of the foliage as possible. Do not overdo it; once the liquid has started to drip off the leaves, move on.
- Store chemicals out of reach of children and where accidents cannot happen, preferably in a locked cupboard. Do not store them under the kitchen sink.

Pruning

Pruning is not the mystery it sometimes seems. There are straightforward rules to follow that will demystify the whole business. First, making the cuts. All pruning cuts are best made just above a healthy shoot, leaf

joint, leaf or bud. Try to make your cut leaving about 3–6mm/⅛–¼in of stem above the bud or joint. Leave too much and the stem will rot; cut too close and the bud may be damaged.

Use a sharp and clean pair of secateurs. Never, ever, use a pruning knife – they can be very dangerous. For shoots thicker than about 12mm/½in, use long-handled loppers rather than secateurs.

Now, which plants to cut and when. It's mainly shrubs and climbers that need regular pruning, together with all tree and bush fruit. It pays to look at your shrubs and climbers every spring when they're growing well and cut out any dead shoots, any especially spindly-looking ones, any that are damaged or split, plus any that are rubbing and creating wounds. This can be a little difficult on plants like clematis and philadelphus with

their masses of twiggy growth, but I'm sure you get the idea.

The purpose of pruning is to create a healthy plant and encourage it to give generously of the features for which you planted it. Most shrubs and climbers are grown for their flowers, but different plants produce flowers on different types of growth. Most roses and buddleias, for example, flower in summer at the ends of shoots that have been growing since spring. Others, like forsythia, flower along shoots that have grown during the previous season.

The idea is to encourage growth that will produce flowers, and as pruning generally encourages growth, plants like buddleias are pruned hard in the spring, just as they start to grow. New shoots develop that will flower prolifically in the summer and autumn. All the

shoots that have flowered the previous year are cut back hard, to within a few centimetres or inches of the really old wood.

If you prune spring-flowering plants like forsythias in early spring, you'll cut off all the flowers just as they're opening. So plants that flower relatively early in the year on shoots that have grown the previous season are pruned immediately after the flowers drop, usually in late spring. So instead of cutting all the

ABOVE: Small trees grown for their bark, like this cherry, are best left entirely unpruned and can even be washed to show off the colour.

OPPOSITE, LEFT: Buddleias should be cut back hard in early spring to encourage strong new growth that will flower profusely.

OPPOSITE, RIGHT: Forsythia flowers on the growth that developed the previous year, so prune shoots that have flowered when the flowers fade.

shoots back very hard, cut back only those shoots that have just carried flowers and leave the new ones to grow on and flower the following spring. Plants in this group include forsythias, philadelphus and flowering currant.

There are also plants that are grown for their foliage, especially variegated and yellow- or purple-leaved shrubs. These are usually simply left to grow naturally, although it's very important to cut out any completely green shoots as soon as they appear. These are more vigorous than the yellow or variegated shoots, and if left in place would soon swamp the whole plant.

A few plants – some dogwoods and willows, for example – are grown for their brightly coloured stems, which are especially attractive during the winter. The aim here is to encourage as many long colourful stems as possible, so these too are cut back hard in spring every year.

Removing branches

Occasionally a large branch needs to be removed from a mature shrub or tree, and there's a right way of going about it. First of all, do not attempt to remove branches from large trees yourself – it can be very dangerous to you and to your house. Call in an expert.

If possible, branches should never be cut off leaving a stump. Try to cut back to another healthy branch. Branches that are easily accessible and over about 5cm/2in across should be removed using the following technique.

Technique

1. Remove much of the lighter growth from the branch using loppers or secateurs to leave a relatively short, more or less bare branch.
2. About 30cm/12in along the branch from where your final cut is to be made, use your saw to make a cut upwards into the branch from underneath. This cut should go about one third of the way into the branch.
3. Just a little farther out along the branch, make a cut from above to remove the branch. The aim is

for the branch to break as the second cut approaches alongside the first; the presence of the first undercut prevents the bark tearing back towards and down the trunk when the branch breaks, which would create a wound.

4. You'll be left with a short stump that can be removed with a cut from above and is light enough for you or a helper to hold, preventing the bark from being torn.

5. The final cut should be just a little proud from the branch to which it is attached.

Making compost

Organic matter, as you'll have gathered if you've read this far, is one of the most crucial elements in successful gardening and it has to come from somewhere. The most sensible place for it to come from is the garden itself, via the compost heap.

Garden compost is simply well-rotted vegetable matter of any kind: annual weeds and the top growth of perennial weeds will make up a substantial part of the mixture, together with outer leaves and peelings from vegetables. Fallen leaves are best stacked separately to make leaf mould, and although some grass mowings can go on the compost heap, they should not make up more than 25 per cent of the whole.

Plastic compost bins keep the heap together, and in a very small garden that yields little waste are quite adequate. However, many gardens and households produce enough waste to feed a larger wooden bin (or even two). The larger size, and the increased insulation of the wood, helps the heap to heat up well, and this heat helps to kill weed seeds and pests.

In a small garden, the flow of suitable vegetable waste for the compost heap may be slow and unpredictable. My advice is simply to fling the waste into the bin as it accumulates and then, as it nears full capacity, to empty

LEFT: Weeds, spoiled vegetables and kitchen peelings can all go on the compost heap, but avoid meats and the roots of perennial weeds.

OPPOSITE: When it's ready, garden compost should be dark, crumbly and sweet smelling - ideal for improving your soil.

the whole thing out and rebuild it properly. In late spring and summer, compost should be ready in just a couple of months. Heaps made in autumn will usually be ready in spring.

To build a heap properly and generate the maximum weedkilling heat, start by setting a few bricks in the base to support 15cm/6in of dry twiggy material (tough perennial stems are ideal); this will let in valuable air. Then fork in 23cm/9in of compost material and top it with a scattering of proprietary compost activator (from the garden centre) or farmyard or stable manure. Next, add another layer of compost material, then more activator. The instructions on the pack of activator may vary slightly from this: follow them. When the bin is full, cover it with a piece of old carpet to keep excess rain out and the heat in.

Feeding

Plants derive their nutrients from the soil and are fed in two ways. The soil itself can be improved so that there's a natural reservoir of plant foods constantly available. This is done by the regular application of organic material. Alternatively, neat plant foods (fertilizers) can be applied to feed the plants directly, and these are gradually dissipated – taken up by plants and washed through by rain.

Most gardeners use a combination of the two methods of feeding. They add organic matter when preparing the soil and when planting, and apply extra nutrients every year or two by mulching (see page 107). In addition, dry fertilizers are applied annually, usually in spring.

Plants in containers, and greedy plants such as tomatoes, are also best fed with a liquid fertilizer during the growing season to promote maximum flower production or yield. Products that are designed for specific crops and groups of plants are available at the garden centre, but a general feed is usually acceptable (see page 95).

Dry fertilizer should be applied evenly, and the granular formulations make this easy. Follow the recommendations – putting on extra can be both

harmful and wasteful. To help apply the fertilizer evenly to new beds and borders, the area to be fed can be marked out in square metre or square yard sections using canes and a garden line. The required amount per square metre or square yard can then be sprinkled on each square.

Lawn mowing

It sounds simple: you push the mower backwards and forwards over the lawn until it's all cut, then you put the machine away. End of story. But like most things, it can be done well or badly.

Safety should be the first consideration. If you have an electric mower, make sure your cable is easily long enough to reach the farthest corner of the area to be cut. If not, use an extension.

To look their best, lawns should be cut every week when growing strongly, less often in dry spells and early and late in the year; they may need cutting right through mild winters. Set the height of cut so the lawn is not scalped, leaving bare soil. The next to lowest setting is usually right for fine lawns; leave it longer on rougher, bumpier surfaces.

Whenever you cut the grass, cut the edges of the lawn too; it will make a dramatic difference to the look of the garden. Using a pair of long-handled edging shears, stand upright with your feet side by side at right angles to the edge. The lower blade should be nearest to the lawn.

Then simply shuffle along, cutting the grass sticking out towards the border with a scissors motion and leaving the clippings where they fall. When you're done, gather up the clippings.

Cylinder mower

Start by cutting one mower width all the way round the edge. Then, if your mower is electric, leave the cable coiled on the newly mown strip at the edge nearest the power source. Mow in parallel stripes from there until you get to the other side.

Wheeled rotary mower

Check to see if the mower cowling has a slight overhang to one side. If so, mow a strip all the way round the lawn with this overhang cutting the very edge of the grass. Then mow in parallel stripes.

Hover mower

It's tempting to use the freedom that the hover system provides to swing the mower around in a freer, less organized way. But you're less likely to run over the cable accidentally if you mow the edges and then in rows as above.

ABOVE: Keep your lawn cut regularly; it will take less time to maintain than cutting much longer grass at less frequent intervals.

OPPOSITE: Spread a general fertilizer on new borders before planting to give the plants a flying start.

Chapter 4

Preventing Problems

The sad fact is that at some time in their lives your plants are going to be attacked by various unwelcome organisms. These may be pests, usually insects or their relatives, although they may be larger creatures; they may be diseases, some of which are so microscopic that you can't even see them; or they may be weeds, which can be invasive wild plants or even garden plants growing too enthusiastically. All is not lost though. Good cultivation techniques together with organic or chemical controls provide an effective arsenal with which to combat these problems.

Prevention

Most plants are attacked by pests and diseases at some time or other, but please don't infer from what follows that gardening is nothing more than a continuous battle against nature's predators.

Preventative measures

Prevention is the best cure, but however diligent you are, problems will arise sooner or later. Vigilance and prompt treatment are the two things that together will ensure that your pest problems never get out of hand. And, of course, both plants and gardeners can tolerate low levels of pests and diseases without suffering unduly.

Following a few simple guidelines will help to keep your plants free from pests and disease.

• Check new plants before buying them as well as presents from friends. It's a wise precaution to spray all new plants, whatever their source.

• Choose pest- and disease-resistant varieties if possible.

• Grow plants in conditions as near as possible to those that suit them best, and that pests and diseases dislike, so that the plants are able to withstand attack.

• Water and feed plants according to their requirements; both too much and too little can weaken them. Keep splashes of water off foliage and flowers to prevent rot from getting a hold.

• Deal with natural reservoirs of pests and disease by clearing rubbish from the garden and keeping weeds down.

• Encourage a wide variety of insects, like hoverflies, lacewings and ladybirds, and other garden wildlife that will help keep pests in balance.

• Prune correctly and at the right time of year, cutting out dead and weak wood if nothing else. Remove dead flowers, leaves and fruits that might become infected with pests and disease.

Organic control

Here I'm using the term 'organic control' to mean any control method except those involving chemicals that are not of natural origin. So it covers the use of chemicals of natural origin, together with manual and cultural techniques.

The simple manual methods are often overlooked. Some pests – caterpillars, for example – can simply be picked off by hand and you can squash the caterpillar eggs that are sometimes found underneath foliage. Pinching off a badly infested shoot and putting it on the fire or in a sealed bag in the bin can often stop pests from spreading. Basic barrier methods using fleece or polythene can also be highly effective.

Pest control using predatory and parasitic organisms is now a familiar concept. They are generally used in one of two ways. Microscopic creatures are mixed with water and watered on to the soil, where they attack soil pests, or slightly larger ones are introduced to the greenhouse as pests start to build up and then either eat the pests or parasitize the pests' eggs.

Encouraging birds into the garden will help with a number of pest problems, but don't forget that some crops, especially fruit, may need protection from birds.

Chemical control

Your first reaction should not be automatically to reach for the spray. Sprays are sometimes necessary but think first. In response to increasing concern from gardeners, chemical companies are now producing far more useful information, and leaflets are often available at garden centres or free from the manufacturers. Always follow the instructions on the pack. In recent years, as safety regulations have become more strict, the number of products available has been reduced dramatically. The situation is continually changing, but for many problems there is no chemical solution.

There are four methods of applying chemicals: spraying, dusting, soil treatment and fumigation. Spraying is the most common, and for a discussion of methods and safety precautions, see page 109. Dusts can be useful as soil treatments but are otherwise rather hit-and-miss, and few are now available.

OPPOSITE: Some problems are not caused by pests or diseases; very dry conditions combined with hot sun can cause leaf edges to turn brown.

Soil is treated in different ways for different problems. Dusts or small granules may be mixed into the soil to deal with soil-living pests that attack roots. Small pins or pellets impregnated with insecticide are available – these are pushed into the compost of pots and containers and release the chemical over a few weeks. These are especially useful for house plants and containers near the house, where you may not wish to spray.

Some liquid treatments are watered on to the soil and are taken up by the plants' roots; pests that suck sap, eat leaves or feed on the roots are then killed. These are often the most effective, and pose the least danger to beneficial insects and other parts of the garden.

Fumigation is used exclusively in greenhouses and conservatories. It consists of using a purpose-made fumigant cone that, when lit, produces billowing clouds of insecticidal smoke that carry the chemical to every corner of the greenhouse and right into the shoot tips of the plants. This is an effective method if the vents on your greenhouse are a tight fit but ineffective and highly antisocial if they are not. Depending on the active ingredient, fumigants usually kill beneficial as well as harmful insects. Never use fumigation in a conservatory or sunroom that is connected to the house.

Pests

Most general pest problems are caused by a limited range of creatures that can be easily controlled in the small garden environment using a combination of good cultivation techniques and organic and/or chemical controls.

Ants

Ants undermine the roots of plants and 'farm' aphids by moving them from one plant to another.
Damage: Drying out, through the removal of soil from roots plus increasing aphid infestation.

OPPOSITE: The larvae of the familiar ladybird is one of the most voracious of greenfly predators; spraying for greenfly will usually kill ladybirds too.

Most susceptible plants: Perennials, rock plants, annuals and lawns.
Organic control: Boiling water poured into the nest is occasionally successful. Be tolerant.
Chemical control: Bait with an ant treatment until all signs of activity have ceased. Treat the honeydew-emitting aphids to discourage the resulting ants.

Aphids

Greenfly, blackfly and others in a variety of colours are the commonest of all pests. There are many different types; some tend to attack specific plants, while others are more omnivorous. There is little hope of prevention, and indiscriminate spraying should be avoided, as this kills insects that feed on aphids.
Damage: Weak growth, deformed shoots and groups of insects under leaves and along shoots.
Most susceptible plants: Annuals, perennials, vegetables, herbs and new shoots of shrubs and fruit trees.
Organic control: Encourage predators, rub off small infestations with fingers and spray infected plants with insecticidal soap. Pay special attention to the undersides of the leaves.
Chemical control: Available and effective.

Birds

Birds can be a mixed blessing in a garden. While they will devour large quantities of insect pests, they will also eat seeds, young flowers and food crops.
Damage: Pigeons can strip foliage; finches eat fruit and flower buds; sparrows peck off the flowers. Many birds eat fruits, and their dust bathing can make holes in newly sown lawns.
Most susceptible plants: Foliage of cabbage family; flowers of crocuses, polyanthus and primroses; flower buds of mahonias, forsythias and cherries.
Prevention: Plant susceptible shrubs in front gardens, where birds may be frightened by passers-by. Crocus and polyanthus can be protected using black cotton tied to sticks and stretched between the plants. Net your food crops. Lay net or twigs on new lawns.

121

Capsids

Damage is seen more often than the creature itself, which is pale green in its larval stage and bright green in its adult form.

Damage: Small, ragged, often yellow-edged holes in tips of shoots, the holes enlarging as the leaves expand.

Most susceptible plants: Perennials, annuals and sometimes shrubs.

Prevention: Clear away plant debris and dry leaves, especially from underneath hedges.

Organic control: Pinch out shoot tips.

Chemical control: Available.

Caterpillars

Caterpillars of a wide variety of moths and butterflies attack the leaves and fruits of a huge range of plants.

Damage: Leaves are eaten, usually from the edge and often giving a characteristic scalloped appearance. Some, usually more specific feeders, eat fruits.

Most susceptible plants: Cabbage family, nasturtiums, columbines and fruit of all kinds.

Prevention: Squash eggs on the undersides of leaves and encourage insect-eating birds.

Organic control: Pick off caterpillars by hand and spray with a parasitic bacterium.

Chemical control: Available and effective.

Leaf miner

This a tiny moth caterpillar is an unexpectedly difficult and disfiguring pest.

Damage: Silvery tunnels in the surface of leaves.

Most susceptible plants: Hollies, chrysanthemums, columbines, marguerites, laburnums and lilacs.

Organic control: Pick off affected leaves.

Chemical control: Difficult, but available.

Red spider mite

This tiny reddish sap-sucking insect is the most difficult common pest to eradicate and is very destructive.

Damage: Delicate yellow mottling of foliage, followed by fine grey webbing on the plants in the greenhouse, conservatory and indoors and, increasingly, outside.

Most susceptible plants: Inside – cucumbers, bougainvillaea; outside – primroses, crocosmia and strawberries.

Prevention: Most prevalent in hot dry conditions, so keep the atmosphere damp in the greenhouse by spraying foliage and dousing paths.

Organic control: Predatory mites can be used to control the red spider mite in greenhouses.

Chemical control: Available, but not completely effective, partly because the mites develop resistance.

Slugs and snails

Slugs tend to be more of a problem on acid soils, while snails are more common on limy soils…but many gardens boast damaging populations of both, in all sorts of colours and sizes..

Damage: Seedlings are eaten off at ground level, new shoots are eaten as they peep through the soil and softer foliage can be eaten all through the season.

Most susceptible plants: Almost any.

Prevention: Both like to hide in cool damp spots, so clear away long grass and weeds and consign all debris to the compost heap. Surround individual plants with a line of grit or lime, which slugs dislike.

Organic control: Various traps can be used, ranging from the old favourite, the saucer of beer, to upturned half-orange or grapefruit skins. Some organic gardeners resort to night-time expeditions with a torch and a tin. Copper bands are available for containers and small planted areas. Some preparations work by causing shrinkage of the creature's slime glands and are simply watered on to the soil; others disrupt reproduction and, although they take time to affect the population, work very well. Neither affects wildlife or other organisms.

Chemical control: Pellets containing methaldehyde are still popular; the blue-coloured mini-pellets are unappealing to animals, and they also usually contain a repellent to deter pets and other animals from eating them. Predators can still be harmed when they eat

OPPOSITE: Caterpillars like this mullein moth can cause a great deal of damage in a short time but are easily picked off the plants.

dying slugs. It's worth remembering that you need very few pellets to do an effective job. You'll find that placing single pellets 10–15cm/4–6in apart is usually just as good as putting fifty in a trap – it's more effective and cheaper too.

Vine weevil

The vine weevil is an increasingly troublesome, and destructive, pest. The white, soil-living grub hatches into a small black weevil.

Damage: Bulbs, crowns of plants, fleshy roots and sometimes juicy stems are chewed by the grubs; plants wilt and die. Mostly seen in containers but increasingly common in the open garden, especially near hedges. Adults takes notches out of the edges of leaves.

Most susceptible plants: Primroses, begonias, heucheras, bergenias, epimediums and sedums.

Prevention: Difficult. The weevil usually arrives on an infected plant but is hard to detect. Dress the tops of pots with sharp grit to deter them from laying eggs.

Organic control: Remove grubs when repotting. Use a parasitic eelworm, which also kills mushroom fly larvae.

Chemical control: Use a long-lasting systemic insecticide that is watered on to the compost or soil.

Whitefly

Clouds of white insects that fly up when you knock against foliage.

Damage: Sap-sucking insects reduce the vigour of plants and drop honeydew on to foliage; this is then infected with black sooty mould.

Most susceptible plants: Inside – tomatoes, cucumbers and primulas; outside – cabbage family and nasturtiums.

Organic control: Biological control with a parasite is very effective in a warm greenhouse.

Chemical control: Sometimes effective, though resistance is a problem. Use a long-lasting systemic insecticide that is watered on to the compost or soil.

OPPOSITE: Aphids are the most common pests and are difficult to prevent, but encouraging predators such as ladybirds can limit infestations.

Woolly aphid

This small brown aphid, which covers itself in white woolly wax, is a branch-living relation of the greenfly.

Damage: Colonies disfigure the bark and cause cracks and fissures through which diseases can infect.

Most susceptible plants: Apples, pyracanthas, cotoneasters, sorbus and other shrubs and trees in the rose family (though not roses).

Organic control: Limited infestations can often be dealt with by painting colonies with methylated spirits.

Chemical control: Available.

Diseases

As with pests, a small number of diseases cause most of the problems. Creating the right growing conditions is even more helpful in preventing disease attack than it is in relation to pests.

Grey mould

Grey mould, or botrytis, is a disease that occurs in damp conditions and is especially common in the autumn and winter.

Damage: Flowers, fruits, leaves and stems turn grey-brown and a white, furry mould develops. It attacks foliage, especially when it's been damaged, and also flowers - dead flowers in particular - together with the stems left after flowers have fallen; it then spreads into healthy tissue quickly.

Most susceptible plants: Wide range, especially double flowers and fruits.

Prevention: In the greenhouse and conservatory water sparingly, avoiding splashing water on foliage and on the floor, and if possible install automatic ventilators. Heat the greenhouse or conservatory with a dry heat such as electricity or a radiator rather than a damp heat from paraffin or gas, which will exacerbate the problem.

Organic control: None.

Chemical control: Available and effective, but improving growing conditions is crucial.

Damping off

Damping off is a disease of seedlings that causes them to collapse at soil level and die.

Damage: A fungus in the compost attacks the young seedlings either as they germinate or at soil level soon afterwards, causing them to collapse. The infection usually starts in one part of a pot or tray, and spreads as the fungus moves through the compost. The fungus is usually introduced on dirty pots or trays, by re-using old compost, and very often in water that is taken from a rainwater tank. It develops and spreads quickly in badly drained compost that has been firmed too hard, or compost that is overwatered.

Most susceptible plants: Seedlings of all kinds, especially small slow-growing ones.

Prevention: Use clean equipment and fresh compost straight from the bag. Don't overfirm compost, especially peat-based types, and don't overwater. If you're raising a lot of seedlings of one variety, sow in two smaller pots rather than one large one so that, if one pot is infected, you still have the other. The disease will also spread less quickly if seed is sown thinly, so that the seedlings are not too crowded when they emerge. As an extra precaution add a copper fungicide to the water when watering.

Organic control: Treat with a copper fungicide, but once the disease is obvious it's often too late.

Chemical control: As above.

Downy mildew

This group of mildews is less obvious than other types; the brown rot that sometimes affects the midribs of lettuce is a good example.

Damage: Soft brown rots with much less in the way of white dust than powdery mildew.

Most susceptible plants: Lettuce, cabbage, spinach, vines, beetroots, onions, peas and more.

Prevention: This group of mildews is encouraged by damp conditions; avoiding overwatering and not splashing water is important.

Organic control: Plant resistant varieties.

Chemical control: Available.

Powdery mildew

Rose mildew and others like it are known as powdery mildews. They are encouraged by hot, dry conditions and are especially destructive in long, hot, dry summers.

Damage: White powdery coating over leaves and flower buds.

Most susceptible plants: Roses, apples, brassicas (especially swedes, turnips and sprouts), cucumbers, gooseberries, peas, strawberries and vines all have their own particular strains of mildew that will not infect other plants. Other plants attacked include dahlias, delphiniums, zinnias and monarda.

Prevention: Careful siting of susceptible plants is helpful. Climbing roses growing on south-facing walls are especially susceptible, so should be planted on walls and fences facing west or east. Resistant varieties can play a part in preventing infection.

Organic control: Pick off the first mildew-affected shoots and keep a humid atmosphere in greenhouses, but if the conditions are right for it, mildew will soon return.

Chemical control: Available, and effective.

Viruses

Virus diseases of plants are becoming increasingly common, and they are almost always spread by soil or flying insects.

Damage: Viruses cause a wide variety of symptoms, including weak growth, poor fruit set, twisted shoots, mottled or streaked foliage, poor yields, difficulties in rooting cuttings and coloured streaks in flowers.

Most susceptible plants: Almost any plant.

Prevention: Viruses are carried from plant to plant by aphids, and a few are carried by soil-borne organisms and by sap left on cutting tools. Controlling the aphids that spread the virus is a big help.

Organic control: Dig up and burn infected plants.

Chemical control: None.

OPPOSITE: In dry seasons, powdery mildew can devastate border phlox, but keeping the plants moist and choosing one of the few resistant varieties will help keep mildew at bay.

Chapter 5

Garden Styles

Settling on a theme for the whole garden or, more often, for certain elements within it, often helps to clarify your ideas, concentrate the mind and encourage effective planning. There are many different styles of garden to choose from. For example, you may prefer a garden that provides seasonal interest, one that attracts wildlife or a garden that looks good but requires very little maintenance. Features such as containers, raised beds, pools and fountains may also appeal. The style you choose will depend on the particular garden you have as well as personal taste.

The seasonal garden

The all-year-round garden is a much discussed ideal but is rarely achieved with any great success. A garden in which all the plantings look good all the year round is an almost impossible dream. The usual result is that the whole garden always looks well furnished, but never looks spectacular.

Planning ahead

There is a way in which you can have a colourful garden all the time – by assigning beds and borders to specific seasons. For example, gather many of your winter-flowering and winter-colouring plants together in a sunny, sheltered spot where you can easily see them from the path or the kitchen window. Similarly, autumn, spring and summer plants can be grouped separately to make striking displays in separate beds, borders or corners, the interest moving around in the garden as the months go by. Of course, an autumn border need not be completely uninteresting in spring; adding a simple undercarpet of dwarf bulbs will create a two-season border.

Some gardeners are tempted to plant their garden, or perhaps just one area of it, to be at its best at a more specific time – to tie in with an anniversary, perhaps, or with a regular summer visit to a holiday cottage. This sounds like a fine idea, but with the seasons becoming increasingly unpredictable, such planning can misfire badly. You may always have a big family party in the first week of July, for example, and like to plan for the area round the patio to be at its best at that time, but an unusually warm spring may bring flowering forward by as much as a month, ruining your plans. It's usually more practical to be less specific and aim for a slightly longer period of colour so that you can be sure that whether the season be early or late there'll still be plenty of colour and interest.

Tulips can be set around spring-flowering shrubs for dramatic early colour and then replaced with summer flowers for later.

Individual plants of these seasonal summer flowers – helichrysums, rudbeckias and phlox – knit together to create a sparkling carpet.

Spring

In an open situation, spring displays can be provided by seasonal flowers like wallflowers, pansies, violas, forget-me-nots and double daisies, planted with bulbs such as tulips and grape hyacinths. The display can be changed each year and can give way to a temporary summer display as they fade in late spring and early summer. Mediterranean flowers and bulbs, mulched with gravel, make a good permanent spring planting. Alternatively, a partially shaded site under fruit trees or in the shadow of next door's oak tree can be given over to spring-flowering woodland plants like primroses, epimediums, pulmonarias, erythroniums, daffodils and other bulbs.

Summer

There's a huge range of plants that can be used for a temporary summer display to follow the spring seasonals, from familiar seed-raised bedding plants such as marigolds, petunias, lobelia and salvias, to the classier tender perennials – argyranthemums, verbenas, gazanias and so on. For permanent plantings there's also a vast range of shrubs, climbers, perennials and bulbs.

Autumn

Autumn flowers go with autumn foliage. Just as the leaves of shrubs turn to orange and yellow, the blue salvias and ceratostigma, the fiery crocosmias and the garden chrysanthemums are also at their best. The more lurid Michaelmas daisies need careful placing.

Winter

A winter border could be based on winter-flowering shrubs, willows and dogwoods for their colourful winter twigs, a few variegated evergreen shrubs and ivies, smaller conifers, snowdrops and aconites, bergenias for their winter foliage and winter-flowering hellebores. In mild climates, of course, there will be more variety to choose from.

Plants such as crocosmias will provide a long season of interest, flowering from summer into autumn; the spikes can also be cut for the house.

The crowded clusters of berries on this cotoneaster last well into winter, and they will then attract birds to the garden.

ABOVE: Gravel mulch over landscape fabric, rocks and boulders, and plants that don't continually shed leaves will all significantly reduce maintenance.

OPPOSITE: The key to creating a cottage garden is to avoid an overly contrived appearance and to let nature take its course.

The low-maintenance garden

Some gardeners love the day-to-day work of caring for the garden, and for many it's part of the point. But for others – be they busy, lazy or with other priorities – it makes more sense to create the most attractive garden with the least possible work. In that case the aim should be to develop boundaries, surfaces and plantings that require the least possible maintenance.

Practical choices

When trying to create a low-maintenance garden it's tempting to overplant evergreen shrubs that need little or no care, smother weeds effectively and always have a presence. This is not the best option, however, because this type of planting reduces the season-by-season change that is such a crucial feature of a small garden. Most plants, shrubs or perennials that are growing well and that were not planted too far apart in the first place will soon make a troublefree weed-smothering cover. And they'll look good too.

Here are a few guidelines to help you plan a garden that requires the least amount of upkeep.

- Plan your garden around hard or gravel surfaces and mixed borders.
- Don't have a lawn.
- Choose robust plant varieties with a spreading habit.
- Do not leave large gaps between plants when planting.
- Mulch all the borders every year.
- Install seephose/soakerhose under the mulch and invest in an automatic timer.
- Add a layer of landscape fabric under all gravel or bark paths.
- Avoid specialist plants like alpines, containers of any kind and seasonal flowers.
- Avoid shrubs like roses and buddleias that need annual pruning.
- Always be sure that the soil is free of perennial weeds before planting.
- Choose perennials that are self-supporting.
- Buy a comfortable sun lounger.

The cottage garden

Most of us have a vague idea of what constitutes a cottage garden: a path from gate to front door, lined with pinks or saxifrages and with a tumble of plants behind - roses, hollyhocks, lupins, foxgloves, sweet peas. There may be a little topiary and a few fruit trees, there'll be plenty of vegetables, and any containers from buckets to Wellington boots will accommodate geraniums or houseleeks.

Basic principles

Cottage gardens have changed a great deal from medieval times, when animals, especially chickens and the pig, were far more important than vegetables. The nineteenth century was probably the heyday of the cottage garden; one unusually enlightened coal-owner actually gave cottagers cabbage plants and fruit bushes from his own nursery, cleared their gardens for them and then awarded prizes for the best-kept plots.

The key to contemporary cottage gardening on a small scale is to treat plants as individuals. It's true that there might be a row of pinks or London's pride (*Saxifraga × urbium*) along a path, but otherwise it's only in the vegetable garden that you'll find more than one or two of the same plant together. Perennials that could be chopped up with a spade and replanted, annuals that self-sowed and roses that could be grown from twigs simply stuck in the ground were the staple plants of the old cottage garden. Although many of the plant varieties that were grown in the nineteenth century are no longer with us and so many newer plants have since been introduced, keeping to these basic ideas will help you create a modern cottage garden with more than a little of the old style.

Choosing plants

You can create a cottage-style planting in sun or shade, in a border or in a bed set in grass, but the most appropriate setting is probably the front garden, where the path can wind through to the front door. Over-careful planning is perhaps the antithesis of the cottage

garden ideal; allowing the plants to behave naturally is part of the art. When it comes to which plants to put alongside each other, it's important to be guided by your own tastes and not to follow the recommendations in this or any other book too closely. The cottage garden approach really does involve letting you and the plants do your own thing without too much interference.

Avoid the most highly developed and highly bred plants, such as F1 hybrid bedding plants, modern hybrid tea and floribunda roses and miniature fruit trees. These may be fine in other situations, but their style is not quite right in a cottage garden. An edging and perhaps a row of espalier fruit trees might be the only concessions to formality, and these will simply mark the back and front of a border. Delphiniums, foxgloves, mulleins, hollyhocks, wigwams of sweet peas and roses on pillars provide height. Annuals and biennials like cornflowers and love-in-a-mist, pansies and sweet william can be allowed to self-sow. Tough perennials like phlox, golden rod, scabious and betony can be left to their own devices for some years, while special campanulas and double primroses need regular division.

The wildlife garden

Small city gardens can provide an invaluable refuge for birds, butterflies and small mammals. Local authorities are incorporating more city parks and verdant verges into their plans, but gardens are still the prime wildlife habitat in many urban and suburban areas.

Assessing your garden

You can encourage many different types of wildlife in a small garden – wild flowers, birds, small mammals, fish, amphibians, butterflies, moths and other insects – but it usually ends up as a series of compromises. After all, a number of butterfly caterpillars feed on stinging nettles, but how big a clump of nettles can a small garden accommodate? How many thistles can you leave to provide seed for finches? How many damp corners can you have for insects? How much grass can you allow to grow long for wild flowers and butterflies? How many rotting logs do you want for beetles and woodpeckers? How big a pond can you have?

Food, water and protection

Birds need nest sites, and the different species have different requirements. A pyracantha is an ideal site for thrushes and blackbirds, and will also have berries later in the year. Birds need water all year round and they need food: fruits and berries, seeds, insects and bird-table food. For many a bird-table will be their only step towards wildlife gardening. Put it where you can see it from the house, perhaps even attached to a windowsill.

Small mammals need cover for nesting and feeding, and they need protection from cats. They need seeds, shoots and other vegetable matter (including your bulbs) or insects to feed on, and their presence is, shall we say, not always compatible with high horticultural standards.

Fish, frogs, toads and newts need water, of course, but they also need protection from herons and sometimes kingfishers, even in cities. Ponds should have a deep area if possible, preferably at least 45cm/18in, with shallower shelves and very shallow areas at the edges. They need floating plants like water lilies to provide shade and marginal plants for cover.

Butterflies need food plants for their caterpillars and these vary from one species to another. The adults require nectar, such as buddleias and sedums. Some need sheltered spots that are cool and dry for hibernation. The variety of conditions that other insects need can usually be provided by not being too rigorous in clearing away garden debris. Native shrubs usually encourage insects more than introduced garden shrubs, but this is far from a definite rule.

RIGHT: Bee keeping is enjoying a resurgence and it's even possible to keep bees in a small city garden.

OPPOSITE: Flowers can be attractive in themselves, like this echinacea, and also add extra delights to the garden by attracting butterflies.

The fragrant garden

So often scent creates an emotional response in us, and we're happy to grow unexceptional-looking plants if they have a scent to which we respond. Night-scented stock is a prime example – its flowers are not even open during the day but that fragrance... That's not to say that a scented garden or scented border need look dowdy, but it's true that some powerfully scented plants are endowed with fragrance to make up for the fact that, when it comes to attracting pollinating insects, their flowers are small or their colours dull.

Positioning scented plants

A garden full of fragrant plants would be a mistake. All those scents would simply mingle and you would end up with no distinctive pleasures. It's also important to remember that plants develop scents in two forms — their flowers may exude scent to attract pollinators, but their foliage may also contain essential oil that is given off when the leaves are rubbed or that vaporizes on very hot days. So, for example, planting rosemary in a sunny position near a path where its aromatic leaves will be brushed against would be a good idea. Here are some guidelines worth remembering to ensure that your scented plants give their best.

- Place scented plants where you can appreciate them fully – by doors and gates, behind or alongside seats, along paths, climbing over arches, by windows that are open in summer.
- Try to separate plants that are fragrant at the same time of year.
- In still air scent lingers, so scented plants are best in a sheltered area and less effective in exposed sites.

ABOVE: Herbs like this rosemary and thyme will thrive in a sunny site and, planted next to a pathway, will fill the air with fragrance as you brush past.

OPPOSITE: Pale coloured flowers complement pale terracotta containers, while plants in richer colours are more effective in dark pots.

Seasons and times of day

A corner of the patio is a fine spot to set a few fragrant plants. However, few of us spend much time relaxing on the patio in winter, so winter plants such as witch hazel, Christmas box (*Sarcococca*) and winter honeysuckle (*Lonicera × purpusii*) are best near the front path. They can be hosts for summer climbers to give colour later in the year.

You'll probably make most use of the patio between late spring and autumn. If you use it in the evening, it is worth remembering that there are some plants whose scent is at its best at this time: herbs with aromatic foliage such as rosemary and sage, scented old-fashioned roses, tobacco plants, jasmine and night-scented stocks. Plants with a more pungent fragrance such as cotton lavender and curry plant are also worth growing – they emphasize the sweeter scents by contrast.

Containers

Most gardens benefit from a few large containers for either permanent or temporary plantings. Fill them with seasonal summer or spring plants and you'll have a regularly changing display that will always be different from the rest of the garden.

Tubs and urns

You can use these containers on the patio, or in any part of the garden that needs livening up, but it's not just the planting of the tubs that justifies their appearance in small gardens. Their very colour and form are so different from most shapes in the garden that they can justify their presence on that score alone. Indeed, some gardens feature large but empty urns for this very reason.

As permanent plants you can use those that demand a soil type different from the soil in the garden itself, varieties that look especially good as isolated specimens or those that are a little tender and need winter protection (they're easily moved to a protected place in the autumn).

Choosing containers

There are numerous different styles and materials to choose from.

- Glazed or unglazed earthenware or stoneware pots and pans (flat or half-depth pots), plain or decorated.
- Reconstituted stone urns in classical or modern styles.
- Glazed urns in various elegant shapes – oriental styles are especially popular.
- Half barrels – in natural colour or painted.
- Concrete planters – cylindrical, dish-shaped, globular or square.
- Timber boxes and troughs – you can make your own.
- Galvanized, stainless or painted steel – boxes or troughs.
- Plastic – the terracotta replicas you can buy now are excellent.
- Found objects – leaky watering cans, wheelbarrows, toilets, old boots, shopping trolleys, chimney pots… Indulge your taste but be prepared for ridicule.

Frost resistance

Many large earthenware pots are imported from countries with hot climates, and the clay may not always be sufficiently pure to survive the rigours of an icy winter. Always inquire about this point before choosing, or buy pots with a guarantee. This is becoming less of a problem, however, as an increasing number are now made with pure clay and, of course, in many areas winter temperatures are becoming less cold.

This is not to say that you shouldn't buy pots that are not guaranteed frost-resistant; simply ensure that they're protected in winter. The obvious thing is to plant susceptible pots with susceptible plants, so that moving them into a porch, sunroom or cold greenhouse in autumn will protect both. Pots that curve inwards at the top are especially prone to damage, and even frost-resistant pots can succumb to an especially harsh winter.

Siting

Large urns make features in themselves and can be sited at the end of a vista, in an alcove framed by evergreens or as the focal point of a formal area. Their size is such that they may have to be left in place permanently.

Pots of a more manageable size can be sited in small groups, though not so close that the individuality of the pots is lost; above a manhole cover is always a good spot. Groups of three pots in a similar style but in a variety of sizes look good together in a corner, and a pair could mark the start of a path. A collection of pots of different styles and sizes, though perhaps in similar materials, makes an interesting display around the back or front door or the door to the summerhouse.

In your first year or two in your new home, when funds may be stretched, large plastic flowerpots can be used. Indeed the quality of some is now so good that, carefully chosen, they can be used as terracotta replicas to make excellent long-term features.

ABOVE: Harmonizing foliage colours can look wonderful; here, hardy perennials and seasonal plants mingle together effectively.

OPPOSITE: Grouping a few large containers can make a striking alternative to flower beds and will be easier to maintain than lots of small pots.

Purpose-made timber planters are ideal for providing planting space where paving or another hard surface cannot reasonably be removed – in a side passage, in corners near doors and so on. They're especially useful in small back gardens with no access except through the house. In these situations, digging up old concrete paving and then improving the soil with compost is often beyond the patience of even the less houseproud, as it will create great inconvenience and be very messy.

However, the materials for large planters can be carried through the house easily, the planters can be built in the yard, and proprietary bagged compost can also be carried through without mess. These large containers can go anywhere, but the compost and plants must be suitable for each other and for the situation.

Maintenance

If built carefully and thoroughly treated with preservative, many timber planters require little maintenance. Just make sure debris doesn't collect underneath, encouraging rotting (and slugs). Planters used for seasonal plantings can be brushed out every year and washed. Timber planters should be painted or treated with preservative every other year. When changing permanent plantings in timber boxes, empty the planter completely, wash thoroughly and allow to dry, then apply a couple more coats of preservative.

Compost

The planting compost you use depends on the plants you intend to grow. In larger containers with a generous capacity, small shrubs and perennial plants will thrive. In this case a rich, soil-based mix is usually ideal, perhaps with extra grit at about 4 parts compost to 1 part grit. If you intend to grow lime-hating plants – dwarf rhododendrons, for example – lime-free, soil-based mixes are available.

Before filling your container with compost you'll need some drainage material. I suggest 2.5–5cm/1–2in of polystyrene packaging pellets, levelled out and topped with a rectangle of green plastic greenhouse shading material or landscape fabric to help prevent the compost from washing through and clogging everything up, and to keep out worms. Packing pellets are much lighter

than the traditional gravel. In very large tubs, use slabs of polystyrene packaging, broken into chunks and topped with pellets and mesh.

Permanent or temporary?

The larger the capacity of your planters the better, as this allows you the option to grow shrubs, perennials and bulbs rather than only small seasonal displays that, in fact, will be happier in containers with less root room. Dwarf evergreen or variegated shrubs, slow-growing conifers, perennials, bulbs and alpines are ideal for larger containers, either home-made or bought.

Some large pots also make good homes for temporary seasonal plantings; the opulence and the exotic air you can create with tender summer tropicals is unmatched by hardy shrubs, and they will look their best in an urn. Smaller pots can be used for just one type of plant, perhaps even an individual specimen, rather than a mixture, whether it's lilies, a scented-leaved geranium, bougainvillea or some special daffodils. These can be brought into prominence as they approach their best, and then removed.

The plants need watering regularly, but a mulch of grit, pebbles, coarse gravel or bark as appropriate will help retain moisture.

Feeding will be necessary too – regular liquid feeding is ideal for temporary seasonal plantings. Permanent plants, especially after the first year, will benefit from a general fertilizer – a handful to the square metre/yard, worked into the surface with a hand fork – each spring before mulching; additional liquid feeds in summer will also be useful.

Window boxes

Many gardeners feel romantic about window boxes, but the number of sad plants you see languishing in them proves that looking after them is not as easy as people like to think.

If you've a mind to, you can buy one of those little plastic boxes and sit it on your windowsill. You can plant it up with busy lizzies and all will be well. Then you can go away for a long weekend, and when you come back

they'll all be frazzled: almost all window boxes sold in garden centres are too small.

There are earthenware and reconstituted stone window boxes that are of a more suitable size, but the only way you can be sure of having one big enough is to make it yourself. Use 23cm/9in (or even 30cm/12in) pressure-treated planks for adequate depth, and brass screws (which never rust) to hold it together. If the sill slopes, you may need to cut slightly wedge-shaped feet to keep the box level.

ABOVE: You can use your window box for a short-season display of berries and foliage for Christmas.

OPPOSITE: In areas with cold climates, this container with its bougainvillea can be moved into a frost-free place for the winter.

Siting and fixing

Window boxes are supposed to be sited in front of windows. Originally they sat on the wide sills in front of the sash windows of nineteenth-century town and suburban houses; the sill was wide enough to support the box and as the window opened vertically the plants could be close to the glass.

Casement windows provide something of a problem: their sills are often too narrow to support boxes and as they open outwards the plants get in the way. Boxes can be set on brackets fixed to the wall below the casement, so that the window opens over the top of the flowers, or the brackets can be set higher in front of windows that don't open. But to be frank, boxes displayed in this way can look silly.

In a small garden details matter, and window boxes in unlikely positions look odd. If you have sash windows and wide sills, window boxes can be very effective in bringing fresh groups of plants and a variety of style to the garden. Otherwise, colour should be introduced around windows by other means, such as hanging baskets at the sides, planting in the soil beneath or the use of large containers set on paving beneath windows.

Even in the more generous root space of a home-made window box, permanent plantings are unlikely to survive in the long term and it's far more effective to use them for two or three changes of temporary planting each year. The main exceptions are dwarf herbs and houseleeks (*Sempervivum*). Twiggy little thymes, in particular, will cope with the limited root space. Houseleeks are ideal and will grow in very shallow compost; their huge variety of rosette colours and colour combinations is interesting all the year round.

Compost

Proprietary container or hanging-basket compost is especially useful for seasonal plantings in window boxes, as it holds more water and holds it for longer than other composts. Use a 2.5cm/1in drainage layer of polystyrene pellets plus the fine mesh plastic greenhouse shading suggested for large containers (see page 140).

With rich compost and regular watering and feeding, seasonal plants grow well in window boxes and the result is that, unless you like the crowded and jumbled look, you need relatively few plants. If this is the case, it will be more practical to buy pot-grown plants that, although more expensive, establish themselves very quickly and may well be in flower when you buy them.

For thymes and houseleeks, a soil-based compost with extra grit or perlite for drainage is suitable.

Maintenance

Regular watering is vital, so it's important to make arrangements with friends or neighbours for watering to be continued if you go away. Feeding will also be necessary – one dose of liquid tomato feed when watering in your new plants and then every week from about six weeks after planting. Regular deadheading is also important, and a little judicious trimming is also very helpful in maintaining the look of your plants.

Judging the time to change the planting for the next season is not always easy. The warmth from the wall will help the plants flower for longer into the autumn, and it can be hard to persuade yourself to rip them out to make way for autumn, winter or spring flowers. You can delay beyond the removal of summer bedding from borders, as the warmth will also help spring-flowering plants establish themselves quickly.

Hanging baskets

In recent years hanging baskets have become increasingly popular. The result has been that not only are there more pretty displays round windows and front doors, but there are also more shrivelled sticks poking out of rusty wire and warped plastic. Without careful and constant attention, hanging baskets are difficult to keep looking attractive. My advice is that if you intend to be away from home frequently or are by nature forgetful or lazy, you shouldn't bother with them. If you have the time and the temperament, hanging baskets can bring variety, new shapes and styles, and new plants to your garden, and that's always welcome in a small space.

Choosing plants

Seasonal plantings come in two, three or even four seasons: the summer display is planted in late spring; the spring display is planted in autumn or late winter; an autumn display can go in for a short time in early autumn; or a winter display can be planted in autumn and replaced by spring flowers in early spring.

For summer choose from dwarf and trailing summer seasonal plants; for spring choose spring seasonals, the tougher spring rock plants and even dwarf bulbs; for autumn and winter use dwarf shrubs like heathers and variegated ivies, which can be removed and planted in the garden when replaced by spring flowers.

OPPOSITE: Grouping wall containers and planting them with one variety, can make an attractive formal display when ground space is limited.

The planting style of your basket should match its setting. In some carefully planned and controlled gardens, baskets planted with a riotous mixture of varieties look out of place and plants of just one variety would be more appropriate. In a more cottagey garden a cool, one-colour, one-plant basket may look contrived, where a mixture of varieties would look just right.

When planting use one plant, or even as many as three, in the centre of the basket, a ring around the edge and another ring, staggered with the first, halfway down the side. This will ensure complete coverage. How you mix them is up to you.

Lining the basket

The traditional hanging basket is a dish- or bowl-shaped wire lattice construction lined with sphagnum moss to improve the look and prevent the compost from falling out. Having gone out of favour, the traditional wire basket is now enjoying a revival. Look for a deep basket that will hold plenty of compost. Sphagnum moss is now more widely available at garden centres and is improving in quality – it should be a bright green shade. Moss is still preferred as lining by most gardeners – it looks good and can be easily parted so that plants can be set in the sides of the basket.

Rigid plastic liners rarely fit the basket exactly, often have no drainage holes, and plants cannot be put through the sides unless you cut holes. The same applies to pressed wood pulp liners that, although not intended to be watertight, often are. Some people use black polythene sheeting and cut drainage holes and planting holes with scissors. These look fine once the plants have bushed out to hide the polythene but not before.

If good-quality moss is hard to obtain, there are sensible alternatives. Green or black plastic shade netting is not stiff; being full of holes it's well drained, and it can also be cut easily for planting through the sides. In

LEFT: Hanging baskets, standard lantanas in pots and seasonal summer flowers help integrate this summerhouse into the garden.

OPPOSITE: Densely planted window boxes (here with petunias, fuchsias and lobelia) will need regular watering and feeding to maintain the display.

When fixing to a brick wall, drill and plug the brickwork and use 5cm/2in brass or stainless steel screws to fix the bracket. Be aware of the height at which the basket will hang. Take into account the length of the chain, the depth of the basket and the plants, which will usually hang down even lower.

It can be tempting simply to screw a hook into a soffit and hang the basket from it. The hook will pull out. If you intend to hang your basket from a pergola or archway, again be aware of the weight and use a stout hook, screwed tightly into a pre-drilled hole.

Maintenance

Watering a basket hanging on a bracket 2.4m/8ft from the ground with a watering can is a little tricky. There are pulley systems available for lowering baskets, but they're not cheap. There are also pump action water containers with a long spout to reach up to the basket, but they hold very little water and are hard work.

Much better are the lances for attachment to hosepipes, which have a hooked top to direct water downwards into the basket. These have a very slow flow, but by unscrewing the handle the governor can often be removed to improve this. However, an effective and economical home-made version can be made simply by tying a 1.2m/4ft bamboo cane along a length of hosepipe with about 30cm/12in spare at the end. This allows you to hold the hosepipe vertically and the hose at the end will droop to one side for watering.

The simplest way to feed the plants is to use fertilizer pellets, which can be put in the compost when you plant the basket and break down over the season, releasing plant foods steadily. But most people opt for weekly liquid feeding from about six weeks after planting. The special feeds available for containers are excellent, or use any general feed or tomato food.

Deadheading is important, as is checking for pests and diseases, but probably the most important thing to do is to turn the basket regularly. If left in the same position all the time, the side next to the wall will become bare and brown. Turn the basket every week and growth will be much more uniform.

unobtrusive black or dull green, it can be cut to fit any shape of basket. There are also foam liners in sensibly dowdy shades, with slits in the sides so that they can be expanded to fit any shape and through which you can plant. Coir liners, in dull green, are excellent: they look good, they allow drainage and the liner can be parted with the fingers to insert plants. The only problem is that birds like to steal the fibres to line their nests.

Fixing

It's imperative that the bracket or hook for your basket be fitted well. A basket full of plants and damp soil weighs a great deal and will fall from skimpy fixings.

You can build a raised bed in the sun and fill it with gritty soil for alpines, or you can build one in the shade and fill it with a highly organic mixture for woodland plants. Alternatively, in any spot where the basic soil is inhospitable, it can be filled with good soil for growing just about anything.

A raised bed can go anywhere, but it's important that the site, the soil mixture with which you fill it and the plants you grow are compatible. In a very small garden most beds are likely to be set at the sides, against boundaries, and the aspect will have a great influence.

Siting

A north-facing bed can be filled with a well-drained but organic rich mixture for growing woodland plants. An east-facing bed can have a less well-drained mixture for the same plants; the plants will have to be tougher, otherwise they will suffer from the early morning sun thawing frosted spring shoots too quickly. A south-facing bed is perfect for Mediterranean plants, and a well-drained soil mixture with a grit mulch is ideal. It would also be good for alpines, the rock plants of the high mountains, that enjoy well-drained soil and plenty of sunshine. A west-facing bed, also with a well-drained soil mix, will suit rock plants.

Beds not backed by walls or fences but sited in the open can be provided with deep, well-drained soil for alpines or herbs, or richer soil for smaller border plants.

Materials

Like the materials for paving and paths, those used for raised beds should suit the surroundings. If you have a stone house, use stone for the raised bed walls. Old bricks (frost-resistant of course) are also good.

Timber is an increasingly popular material and blends well in many situations. Short pressure-treated poles are available that can be knocked in vertically to retain the

Raised beds

Raised beds are valuable in small gardens. They bring the plants closer to your eye, which is useful when there'll naturally be a tendency to grow small plants. The variation in level adds variety and a change of style without taking up any extra space. The extra height gives you the opportunity to grow plants in good soil if the soil at ground level is, for example, soaked with oil, full of hardcore or simply rocky. And you don't need to bend so far down – helpful if your back troubles you.

Assessing the possibilities

Raised beds enable you to grow plants that would not otherwise grow in your soil. Look on a raised bed as a giant container that can be filled with any special compost you like, and the possibilities are endless.

ABOVE: A raised bed behind a rough stone wall allows plants that require good drainage to be grown on naturally wet soil.

OPPOSITE: Raised beds also allow vegetables and other food crops to be tended conveniently, a boon for gardeners who find it difficult to bend.

soil, and these are especially useful if you have to cope with changing levels. Half-poles, sometimes known as logroll, are also available stapled to a wire support, making a timber roll that can be bent to fit curves. These half-poles are also available in rigid straight runs.

Wherever you use poles it pays to line them with heavy-duty black polythene to prevent soil from filtering through any cracks. Tree trunks about 15–20cm/6–8in thick are also sometimes used to retain raised beds, but as they're difficult to treat with preservative they have a relatively short life. In modern designs, pressure-treated boards stained an appropriate colour and set on edge can look superb.

Preparation

If you're making your retaining walls from mortared stone or brick, solid footings are important to create stability. For dry stone walls, compacted hardcore will be sufficient, plus a row of especially large flat stones for the first layer.

For railway sleepers, no special preparation is required save compaction of the soil. For individual poles, no preparation is required, while for logroll it's advisable to dig out a trench just a couple of centimetres or inches deep along the line of the logroll and fill it with gravel so that the cut ends of the timber rest on a well-drained medium to help prevent rotting. The same is true of stained boards.

All retaining walls and timber should be erected before the soil is prepared. You should aim for a depth of at least 30cm/12in of soil mixture, even if your raised bed is a low one of only 23cm/9in. It's important that drainage be good, and for rock plants or Mediterranean plants allow for at least 7.5cm/3in of hardcore plus 5cm/2in of coarse gravel unless your soil is naturally gravelly. On top of this lay a sheet of porous landscape

fabric to prevent soil from blocking the drainage. Your soil mixture can go on the top.

For beds where good drainage is less necessary, simply removing any soil to leave enough room for the correct depth of soil mixture and then forking over the existing soil to allow for free natural drainage will be sufficient.

Construction

Brick retaining walls for raised beds should be 23cm/9in thick unless they're fewer than four courses of bricks high. With taller walls it's advisable to incorporate seep holes in the bottom course of bricks by simply leaving the mortar out of every third vertical joint. Dry stone walls should be laid so that they slope downwards slightly on the bed side for extra stability and so that rain water drains back into the bed.

Railway sleepers can be laid on edge to make a bed about 23cm/9in high. If you wish to use sleepers for a higher bed, lay them on their sides rather than their edges. Sleepers laid on edge can be retained in position by rustic poles knocked in on the open side. Alternatively you can knock in some 10 x 10cm/ 4 x 4in posts on the inside to a level about 7.5cm/3in below the surface of the topmost sleeper, drill through post and sleeper, and bolt the two together. Sleepers laid flat are best secured by drilling vertically through them all at the corners where the ends overlap and knocking in a steel rod so that about 15–18in (38–45cm) penetrates the soil beneath.

Rustic poles are simply knocked in to a depth of half their length, protecting the top of each pole with a piece of scrap timber. Logroll is secured in place every 60–90cm/2–3ft by knocking in vertical 7.5 x 7.5cm/ 3 x 3in posts and screwing them to the logroll.

Soil mixtures

Sometimes you'll have spare soil in the garden to form the basis of a mixture for your raised bed – if you're also digging a pool, for example. But this is not always the case and if, for example, your soil is limy and you want

to build a bed for lime-hating plants, your present soil will be useless.

If you're able to utilize some of your own soil, what you add to it will depend on the type of soil you have; it's difficult to be precise about quantities. You'll need grit for drainage, and composted bark, a branded soil improver or other organic matter to retain moisture. For example, I made a raised bed for alpines using 2 parts of my rich, neutral but well-drained soil, 1 part grit and 1 part composted bark (all by volume). For another raised bed for heathers I used equal parts soil and composted bark. Heavier soils would demand extra grit.

Raised beds in small gardens may themselves be quite small, so buying ready-made compost is also a possibility. For a raised bed for lime-hating plants, ericaceous compost is ideal; ask for a discount on a large purchase. For a raised bed for alpines, soil-based John Innes potting compost makes a good base, mixed 3 parts compost to 1 part grit.

Fill your raised bed, treading well as you go and taking special care with dry stone walls to ensure that the mixture fills all cracks and crevices. Fill to the top, but do not plant up your new bed straight away; try to leave it for a couple of months to allow it to settle, topping up with more mixture if there's any sinkage. Patience may be a virtue but is still rare; so, if necessary, treading the bed carefully will allow prompt planting.

Planting and mulching

Try to assemble your plants in good time so that you can plant up most of the bed in one go. Set the plants out on the surface where you intend to plant them, and move them about until you have them in the right positions. After planting, water in well. With alpines or Mediterranean plants especially, check throughout their first summer that they do not dry out.

After planting and watering in, mulching is sensible. For subjects requiring a well-drained compost, a

OPPOSITE: A series of retaining walls is an effective way of dealing with a sloping site and can help create a wonderfully colourful display.

mulch of grit is ideal; for lime-hating plants use a proprietary mulch, composted bark or bark chips; for less demanding plants, any weed-free organic matter is suitable. All mulches will help prevent weed growth and conserve moisture. Grit also takes moisture away from the crowns of susceptible plants and prevents low-growing flowers from being splashed.

Planting themes

Any planting theme suitable for a garden will also be suitable for a raised bed, just on a smaller scale. For specific plant recommendations, see page 208.

Rock plants (alpines) Full sun or west-facing; well-drained soil.

Woodland plants North-facing with well-drained but water-retentive soil; east-facing with slightly less drainage; under tall or sparse deciduous trees.

Lime-hating plants Partial shade; lime-free compost.

Mediterranean plants Full sun or south-facing; well-drained soil.

Herbs Full sun or west-facing; well-drained soil.

Vegetables Preferably full sun, or partially shaded from the side and not from overhead except in hot climates.

Grey foliage plants South- or west-facing; well-drained soil.

Heathers and conifers Full sun, east- or west-facing or an open position; lime-free compost.

Bulbs Full sun; well-drained soil.

Dwarf shrubs and dwarf perennials Full sun, partial shade or east- or west-facing; improved garden soil.

Maintenance

Watering will be the priority in the first six months. Drainage in raised beds is always better than in the rest of the garden, so you'll have to be prepared for watering in hot summers. If you use bought, bagged compost, weeding will not be a problem whether or not you use a mulch. A mix based on your garden soil will produce weeds, especially if you fail to remove all the roots of perennial weeds, which will grow through any mulch. The mulch should be renewed every spring or autumn when the soil is moist.

Water features

Water is an invaluable asset, bringing sound, wildlife and a unique range of plants to the garden. Even on the smallest scale a pool or fountain is worth considering. Now that small pumps, solar-powered pumps and interesting fountain designs are available, you can make a simple water feature in even the smallest space. Site the water with seating areas and near to the house, so that it provides as much enjoyment as possible.

Safety

In a small garden, and especially where there are young children, safety is a crucial consideration, but there are ways of incorporating water into a garden without creating a hazard. The feature could have no open water at all, open water can be covered with sturdy netting, or the area of water can be so small as to pose no danger. On the smallest possible scale, water can tumble through a series of small containers or a water garden can be created in a container as neat as a small half-barrel. Miniature water lilies are now available that will thrive in such a small container.

Perhaps the safest type of water feature is a pebble fountain with no open water. The fountain spills its water into a tank that is filled with large smooth pebbles through which the water drains to be recirculated by the pump. The advantage of this system is that you can have the sound, atmosphere and even some of the plants associated with water, but without danger to children.

The only other relatively safe water feature would be a small stream or series of bowls from which water falls, all powered by an electric, perhaps solar-powered, pump, with little or no open water. Such a feature can be freestanding, built into rockwork or run in a rill across or alongside a patio, with a tank completely hidden below ground. Pre-packaged solar-powered water feature kits are becoming increasingly available.

OPPOSITE: You don't need a large pond to grow water lilies; dwarf varieties can be grown in a very small pool in a very small space.

Until your children are older I would not suggest any other type of water feature unless the surface is completely covered with wire. Pools up to about 90cm/3ft across can be made safe by covering them with stout wire mesh; if you paint it black, it's relatively unobtrusive. The mesh must be heavy-duty and securely fixed to the surrounding brickwork.

Pools

Pools can be formal or informal in shape. In a very small garden a formal rectangular pool is the simplest to build, and pre-formed fibreglass liners are available in various sizes and depths. Round fibreglass liners are also available, and if you want a circular pool this is the best option – fitting a sheet of butyl lining to a round shape will drive you crazy. Pre-formed fibreglass liners are also available in various other informal shapes, and these are often best fitted into a paved surround.

In informal areas pools in a variety of shapes and sizes can be constructed, using butyl liners that can be arranged to fit any pattern. They can be integrated with a small bog garden to enable you to grow marginal plants.

Siting a small pool

Pools can be sited anywhere away from overhanging trees, and although those with a large volume of water are usually best sited in an open sunny position, very small pools and barrels will heat up too much in all-day sunshine; small water features are best sheltered from the sun for at least half the day. Bubble fountains and other features with no standing water can be sited anywhere.

Liners

Liners come in two types – rigid fibreglass and flexible butyl. Polythene sheeting liners are also available, but although much cheaper than butyl, they have a limited lifespan and are best ignored. Rigid fibreglass liners are ideal for smaller pools, especially for a formal pool on a patio, and are now available in grey and dark brown in addition to the rather garish blue that many people dislike.

There's a simple way to calculate the size of the liner you need to order. Take the maximum length of your proposed pool and add twice the maximum depth; then take the maximum width and add twice the maximum depth. This will give you the correct dimensions. There's no need to allow for any overlap at the edge, as the natural stretch of the material will give you enough.

Rigid liners

A pre-formed liner can simply be laid on the ground and marked around to give the size of hole you need to excavate. Excavate the hole for a rigid liner about 15cm/6in bigger all round, firm the base well, and lay 2.5cm/1in of soft sand to provide a cushion for the liner. Make sure the liner is completely supported on the sand base and carefully check that it's level, using a spirit level. Put a little water in the pool, then start to fill the gap between pool and soil with sand, making sure it is worked under any shelves. Fill the pool with water in stages, packing the gap with sand as you go.

Butyl liners

To set out the site for a butyl liner, choose a warm day and lay a hosepipe on the ground to mark out the area you want your pool to cover (hosepipes are more flexible in hot weather).

The correct minimum depth at the deepest part of the pool can be determined by the following guide:
• under 2sq m/25sq ft – depth 38cm/15in;
• 2–9sq m/20–100sq ft – depth 45cm/18in.
The sides of a pool should slope at an angle of approximately 20° – that is, 7.5cm/3in inwards towards the centre of the pool for every 23cm/9in of depth. A shelf for marginal plants should be constructed at a depth of 23cm/9in and should be about 23cm/9in wide.

It seems an obvious thing to say, but it's vital to ensure that the top of the pool is level otherwise the water will run out. Check with a spirit level – then check again.

After careful excavation to the size, shape and slope you require, the bottom and sides should be covered

with a 12mm/½in layer of soft sand to make a smooth surface and protect the liner from stones. If your soil is very stony, an inner lining of polythene matting or old carpet is advisable.

Lay the liner loosely in the hole with an even overlap on all sides, and put a few bricks or pieces of clean timber around the edge to keep it in place. Start to fill the pool slowly with water, stretching and overlapping the liner where necessary to fit snugly into place. Do not hurry this part of the operation – you don't want to have to empty the pond and start again if it goes wrong. When the pool is full, trim off any surplus liner leaving a 15cm/6in flap.

Planting

The simplest way to plant a pool is to use plastic mesh planting baskets. These can be positioned on the shelf or on the bottom of the pool, according to the plants they contain. Different plants require different depths of water over the top of their roots. The correct depth can be provided by utilizing the different depths on the bottom of the pond and on the shelf, and by supporting planting baskets on bricks of an appropriate size (don't use concrete blocks, which leach lime into the water).

As a rough guide, a pool can cope with one water lily for every 2.25sq m/25sq ft of water, although lilies now come in such a variety of sizes that there are plenty of options. Water lilies are unhappy in pools that also feature a splashy fountain. Marginal plants require anything from constantly wet soil but no covering of water, up to a water depth of 45cm/18in, depending on the type. Oxygenating plants, which are vital to keep the pool well supplied with oxygen, will grow in anything from 0.3 to 1.2m/1 to 4ft of water and you need one bunch for every 0.2sq m/2sq ft of water surface.

ABOVE: In gardens with young children, a water feature without open water will provide safety and peace of mind for parents.

OPPOSITE: A rubber pond liner can quickly be disguised using dry stone walling and a simple pump installed to provide sound and movement.

Stocking your pool

A rough and ready guide as to how many fish a pond will comfortably take is 5cm/2in of fish for every 0.1sq m/1sq ft of water surface. It follows that in very small pools and barrels it's impractical to keep fish at all. If you have more fish than the water can take, their waste products will tend to sour the water.

After planting, pools should be left for two to three weeks to settle down before fish are introduced. Before being released, the fish should be floated in the pool in a tied plastic bag full of water to accustom them to the new water temperature. Also, use a water conditioner in the pool water to help the fish acclimatize. The easiest fish to look after in a small pool are goldfish, shubunkins and golden rudd. Golden orfe tend to be very shy if

you have only one or two. As well as fish, ramshorn snails are valuable for clearing up debris and swan mussels are useful to filter algae. Neither is likely to thrive in the smallest pools.

Fountains and pumps

Fountains and waterfalls should not be supplied by constant mains water that simply runs away into a drain; this is wasteful and, if you're on a meter, expensive. Instead a submersible pump should be used to recycle the same water. Low-voltage pumps are safer than pumps run on mains supply. The pump sits in the bottom of the pool, a twin-core cable runs out of the pool to a transformer in a nearby garage or shed, and this is connected to the mains. In most small pools the smallest, lowest-capacity pump is sufficient.

If providing power is a problem, solar power kits are now available that will provide low-voltage power from a panel sited near the pool. These small solar panels need sunshine to drive the pump, and pumping will cease as soon as cloud passes over or the panel is shaded by a tree or the house. Even simpler, and more affordable, are self-contained floating fountains with built-in solar panels. They float free on the water surface and in sunshine provide a fountain about 30cm/12in high.

The only maintenance the pump will need is regular cleaning of the filter. Remove it from the pool and store it inside in winter; this is the time for a 10-minute, do-it-yourself maintenance check, and the literature that comes with the pump will note if this is necessary. Spare parts are available for most models.

A wide range of fountain-heads is available, including aerator heads that oxygenate the water and bell fountain-heads, as well as more conventional types. These are simply fitted to the pump of your choice to give the effect you prefer.

LEFT: Don't be afraid to spend a little time and imagination creating a special water feature; this one is safe for children.

OPPOSITE: Use busy lizzies to enliven a shady situation in summer, while pachysandra and other permanent plantings do duty for the rest of the year.

Woodland features

Many of the most delightful spring-flowering plants grow naturally in the dappled shade and leafy soil of deciduous woodland. This makes them ideal candidates for a small, shady garden.

Creating your feature

Leaf mould can be difficult to come by in large quantities, so moss peat has generally been used instead. However, as gardeners have become more concerned about using peat in the garden, various peat substitutes have been assessed; composted bark seems to be the best alternative, being both widely available and suitable for woodland plants.

A woodland bed is usually made up of one or a series of raised beds filled with woodsy soil. The place where the beds are to go should be marked out and then dug over to allow good drainage, because although one reason for using composted bark is to keep the soil

moist, it should never be waterlogged. Little other preparation is needed before you start work.

Siting

A woodland bed should be sited either on the shady side of a wall or fence or under deciduous trees. If sited on the shady side of a fence, a woodland bed could still get too much sunshine in midsummer when the sun is at its highest and fiercest, so the more delicate varieties may not thrive. Be aware that some trees, like oaks, tend to root deeply and so provide relatively little root competition for woodland plants compared with shallow-rooted, water-grabbing maples.

If a woodland bed is made in the shade of a tree, conifers must be avoided; certain deciduous trees such as beech and horse chestnut cast a very deep shade. Only if the trees are tall and their lowest branches some distance above the ground should a woodland bed be made in such a situation. If you are blessed with such conditions, you should rejoice: the canopy will keep the sun off when it's at its hottest but the slanting rays of the morning and evening sun will still penetrate – ideal.

If you build a woodland bed around a tree trunk, soil should not be banked up against the trunk to a height of more than 30cm/1ft or the tree may suffer. Instead, build a back to the bed – any rough but stout timber or old bricks can be used, as they will not be visible when the plants are in. Corner sites are often the most successful, as they allow you to build a smaller high tier for creeping or pendulous plants and you can incorporate a few steps to allow access.

Materials

Woodland beds are often made in tiers, perhaps with a narrow path to the top to allow close inspection of the smaller, more delicate plants. Various materials can be used to retain the soil and build up the levels. Stone, brick and other materials suggested for raised beds can be used, but timber fits in better. Stout boards such as scaffolding boards, can also be used as well as logs. Logroll can look good in modern situations.

Natural logs are the easiest material to deal with and look the most fitting; they may be available from tree surgery companies. The white bark of birch logs is looks good but soon rots, so use harder woods if possible. Logs can also be used to build the risers of the steps, and the treading area can be filled with bark chips.

Building

Start by laying an edging of logs to mark the main outline. For stability, the logs can be sunk into the soil to about a quarter of their thickness or supported by stout pegs. They look best in single layers, partially buried, and if you can find logs 20–23cm/8–9in across these are ideal. Use a bow or chain saw to cut them all to the right shape and treat generously with clear or brown wood preservative (not creosote, which is dangerous to plants). Having laid your first line of edging and secured it in place, fill the whole area with compost and firm it down. The next layer of logs can then go into place making a second tier, and a small third tier can be built at the back.

Even if a path is incorporated into the design, it's often difficult to reach all the plants to look after them. Stepping stones made with rounds of treated timber cut from logs 30–38cm/12–15in across can be set in appropriate spots before planting.

Soil

The compost used should not be entirely organic. Use a mixture of 2 parts composted bark, 1 part acid-free grit and 1 part good garden soil (by volume). If leaf mould is available (it is sometimes seen bagged in the garden centre), use it to replace some of the bark.

Planting

The compost will be acid, so rhododendrons, azaleas and other lime-hating plants can be grown, although if the underlying soil is limy this will eventually seep into your new compost. Apart from the azaleas and dwarfer rhododendrons, together with related acid-loving shrubs like vacciniums, gaultherias and dwarf pieris, you can also grow woodland plants like primroses, wood anemones, hardy cyclamen, trilliums, lilies and primulas.

Planting is best carried out in spring, and plants may need careful watering in their first year. To top off the planting, create an attractive surface and help prevent weeds, a 2.5cm/1in mulch of composted bark is ideal.

gravel helps to reduce evaporation from the soil substantially. Gravel gardens are best in an open, sunny situation, perhaps with shelter from east winds.

Preparation

Remove all perennial weeds either by digging them out or by using a weedkiller. If soil fertility is poor, fork in some well-rotted compost, soil improver from the garden centre or other organic matter. If the soil is heavy and poorly drained, 2.5cm/1in of gravel can be spread over the surface and forked into the top few centimetres or inches of soil. The area should then be firmed by treading, and a light dressing of general fertilizer – 30g per sq m/1oz per sq yd – raked in.

Construction

On a slope, pieces of natural stone can be used to retain soil and the gravel can sweep around the ends. Stone can also be used on a flatter surface to break up the look. Otherwise, all you need to do is spread 2.5cm/1in of gravel over the whole area. A good guide is that 1 tonne, laid 25mm deep, will cover about 34sq m (1 ton, laid 1in deep, will cover about 45 sq yds). Sometimes gravel may be measured by the 'load', an unhelpfully variable quantity.

Gravel features

Many plants grow well in gravel, and gardeners find that if they have a gravel path or drive, plants will self-sow along the edge. Pea gravel makes a wonderful background for low shrubs, creeping perennials, bulbs and many sun-loving plants.

Creating your feature

An area of gravel can be a very attractive and labour-saving feature. Many slightly tender plants that would otherwise not survive the winter will thrive under the protection of the gravel mulch, and in hot summers the

Planting

Mediterranean plants are ideal for gravel gardens, especially shrubs like cistus, lavender and rosemary. Dwarf bulbs such as iris and crocus do well in gravel, as do helianthemums, the hardier osteospermums, dianthus and perennial wallflowers. Hardy annuals, such as Californian poppies, annual lupins and love-in-a-mist, will usually self-sow generously.

Planting is best done in spring, except for spring-flowering bulbs, which should be planted in the autumn. Do as much of the planting as possible after the soil has been prepared but before the gravel mulch is applied. When plants need to go in later, just scrape the gravel away, put the plant in place with a little extra gravel mixed in for good drainage, and smooth it all over afterwards. Thorough watering is vital.

ABOVE: A gravel path contained by a neat edge makes an attractive and practical walkway among these vegetables, or indeed any plants.

OPPOSITE: In very shady sites, use contrasting foliage plants such as asarums to provide long-lasting interest - flowers need more sun to thrive.

Maintenance

Weeds must be hand-pulled or given a spot treatment of weedkiller as soon as they appear. Clear up in the autumn, when old flowering shoots and any blown leaves that have accumulated around the plants should be removed. Leave most of the cutting down until spring, except where spring bulbs are planted, as the foliage helps to protect tender roots from severe frosts. Rake the gravel to leave it looking neat and to make a good background for early spring bulbs.

A gravel garden that is almost maintenance-free can be created by laying landscape fabric on the soil after preparation; weeds will not usually penetrate the fabric, so maintenance is almost eliminated. Sun-loving shrubs are then planted through the fabric, watered in, and gravel is laid on top of the fabric to provide a neat and attractive finish.

Special plant collections

Sooner or later most gardeners develop enthusiasms for particular groups of plants. I like Mediterranean plants and woodland flowers, while for many years my father grew almost nothing but fuchsias.

Collections for small gardens

There's a great deal of satisfaction to be had from taking a special interest in a limited group of plants. In a small garden, collections of dwarf bulbs, hostas, grasses, pinks, clematis, lavenders, primroses, heucheras, and ferns can all be integrated with other plants. Collections of native plants are also popular. Scented-leaved pelargoniums make good collector's plants for containers, if you have somewhere to store them in the winter.

Collect different varieties, discover their requirements, look into their origins and, in a small garden, work out how a collection can be integrated into the rest of the garden.

Roses

A rose collection takes up a great deal of room, for few roses are small plants and they need their space if they are to flourish. However, some owners of small gardens eschew almost all other shrubs for the sake of growing as many roses as possible. In addition to bush roses, climbing roses can be grown up walls and fences and through shrubs and small trees to add to the range. Beds of hybrid teas are rarely suitable; they look too gawky – shrub roses usually fit best into crowded beds and borders. Miniature, dwarf and ground-cover roses are appearing in an ever-increasing range of varieties, and it's possible to build a collection of these in a relatively small space – although they are not, in themselves, particularly elegant plants.

LEFT: Gravel is ideal if you want a low-maintenance garden. Lay landscape fabric beneath it to keep weeds at bay.

OPPOSITE: Intermingling climbing roses on an attractive wall will allow you to grow more than one rose in the same place.

Alpines

Alpines, often known as rock garden plants, are perhaps the ideal enthusiasm for the owner of a small garden, as they themselves are small and a large collection can be grown in a small space. Many of them, by definition, are also very tough and withstand cold weather. Most alpines need an open sunny situation and well-drained conditions. Finding such a site is not always easy in a small plot, so woodland plants, which are often grown by alpine enthusiasts, may be more appropriate.

The simplest way to grow alpines is in raised beds, while old stone troughs, or their newly manufactured equivalent, are ideal for the smallest species. A few small terraced beds as described for woodland features (see page 155) can look very attractive. Most alpines flower in the spring, but the season can be extended

by seeking out those that flower later in the year and also by growing dwarf bulbs, many of which flower in the autumn. Dwarf shrubs and the occasional very dwarf conifer can add structure and colour in the bleakest months.

Foliage plants

In a sense, all plants are foliage plants, for all plants have foliage. But it's important to recognize that plants with patterned or colourful foliage can make a valuable contribution to the total effect of a garden. This is especially true in a small garden, where it's important that every square metre or yard adds something to the overall impression for as much of the year as possible. By choosing plants that have colourful foliage for much of the year, in addition to attractive flowers, you can ensure that they still contribute something even when not actually in flower. Good examples are *Weigela florida* 'Variegata', *Buddleia davidii* 'Harlequin', *Hosta* 'Honeybells', *Ajuga reptans* 'Variegata' and hardy cyclamen.

Variegated plants come first to mind, for there's a huge range of plants with leaves that are striped, edged, speckled or blotched in white, cream, yellow, pink or gold. They excite strong opinions on both sides, as some gardeners detest them. But if you also consider those plants with yellow, gold, blue, grey, silver, purple, bronze or coppery foliage, plus those with prettily patterned combinations of colours, especially bold, lacy or sword-like foliage or leaves in other striking shapes, you have an enormous collection of possibilities from which to choose.

Some gardeners specialize in grey and silver foliage plants, most of which like sunny, well-drained conditions, or in variegated plants, which are often more adaptable. But any small garden will benefit from the use of colourful and patterned foliage.

ABOVE: A grass collection makes an elegant and easy-to-maintain feature that looks good for many months and even in winter.
OPPOSITE: Heaths and heathers are ideal for a small collection. Hardy and low-growing, they make an interesting tapestry of colour and texture.

Chapter 6

Stocking the Garden

The choice of plants is important in any garden, but particularly in a small garden where space is obviously limited. It's not just a case of buying plants that you like the look of, but of selecting plants whose shapes, colours and textures will work well together in close proximity. There are several ways to stock your garden: you can buy plants from garden centres and other sources; you can propagate them from existing stock or that of friends and neighbours if they are agreeable; or you can sow seeds that you have bought or collected yourself.

Planting schemes

Many expert gardeners know how to care for plants so that they grow well, but not all of them have attractive gardens. The secret is in knowing how to use plants so that they look good together, so that the whole display looks better than simply a collection of plants. In a small garden this is especially important, for every tiny space has to be encouraged to give its best and provide continuing interest and appeal.

Plant associations

There are two different aspects to plant associations. First, fitting in as many plants as possible so that there is always foliage, at least, and if possible flowers, to be seen. Second, giving consideration to how all the shapes, colours and textures will look together. This is the real art, but it's not an art that you have to be born with and neither is it a strange mystical pursuit – it can be learned, and it's not difficult. Some people equate it with planning the decoration and furnishings in the house; they think of it as decorating the room outside. But of course the garden boasts one unique factor: constant change. Not only is every season different, with plants coming to their peak and then fading, but every day is different as buds unfurl or leaves turn gold in autumn. And then there's the weather…

Maximizing your space

There are many ways in which you can grow more plants than you think in a bed or border.
- Grow climbers and wall shrubs on fences and walls.
- Sow annual climbers like sweet peas and canary creeper to grow up wall shrubs.
- Train clematis and other climbers to grow through mature shrubs, as they do naturally.
- Plant climbing roses to grow through trees.
- Plant bulbs among border perennials and ground-cover plants.
- Plant dwarf bulbs and dwarf annuals in the edges of gravel paths and drives.
- Plant bulbs flowering at different seasons among each other.
- Plant tall, late-flowering plants behind earlier flowering plants; they will tend to fall forward and fill the space left when the early ones die back.
- Do not plant perennials with large gaps between them in the mistaken belief that plants must be separate.

Flowers

Flower colour is the feature that comes to mind first, and bringing colours together so that they look good is the main aspect, sometimes the only aspect, of plant association that many gardeners keep in mind.

LEFT: Small borders often look more interesting when their plants are intermingled, like these primulas, poppies and zantedeschias rather than planted in bulky clumps.

OPPOSITE: Coloured-leaved sages and silvery santolinas make an all-year-round foliage display that is also aromatic.

Of course, you have to make sure that plants whose flower colours you feel will go well together do actually bloom at the same time. This can be a little more difficult than you'd expect, as plants vary in their response to changes in weather conditions. Plants that flower in April in more severe regions may flower in February in areas with mild winters. Your own experience will guide you, and you should never be afraid to move plants if planned schemes don't quite come off; it's like scraping the paint off the canvas and starting again.

We all know the red, white and blue of old-fashioned parks bedding, but these same colours can seem unexpectedly stylish if presented by unfamiliar plants in a more intricate style. Other good contrasts include sparkling white against bronze, pale primrose against rich purple, and bright blue with butter yellow. Bringing rich and vibrant colours together is now all the rage: fiery orange and purple, and magenta and lemon…don't be afraid to be bold.

Mixing pastel colours is another possibility. Soft rose-pinks and pale sky-blues look well together, perhaps with white flowers or silver foliage. Lilac and pink look good; pale blue and primrose too. Try using the same colour in different strengths: white flowers and silver foliage; fiery red, orange and yellow; pale sky-blue with deep blue.

Sometimes it's the individual flowers that make the impact; sometimes it's the flower heads, each made up of many small flowers. They come in a great variety of shapes and sizes and you can have fun with them: putting daisy flowers in different colours together is subtle, but setting stiff spikes of flowers with flat flower heads or emerging from a foam of flowers is much more striking.

Foliage

You'll be looking at foliage for a lot longer than the flowers, but that doesn't mean that you should pack your borders with variegated plants. There's so much variety in green foliage alone that you need only a few variegated or silver-leaved plants as highlights.

Variegations come in white, cream, yellow and gold. The colour may edge the leaves, or appear as a central splash or as mottling; there may be stripes in all these shades, as well as spotting and speckling. The whole leaf may be yellow or gold. Silver and grey, when it appears,

usually covers the whole leaf, though there are some plants where additional mottling or spotting occurs. You can tone in flowers with these variegations in the same way as you can colour-match flowers with each other.

Fruits

Fruits and berries are a valuable and colourful feature of the autumn scene, and you can sometimes create a happy association within a single plant. Many mountain ashes and berberis, for example, have fiery autumn leaf colour at the same time that their berries are at their most colourful. Fruits on shrubs like pyracanthas and cotoneasters can be fronted by hardy chrysanthemums in appropriate shades, and many autumn fruits associate especially well with foliage that takes on autumn tints.

Stems

Some plants have colourful stems in winter. To create the best stem colour – red, orange, yellow, green or purple – the plants are cut down hard in the spring to encourage plenty of new growth, which provides the best colour. This also has the effect of keeping the plant small.

The red stems of *Cornus alba* 'Elegantissima' associate well with white-variegated euonymus and the dark, fingered foliage of the stinking hellebore, *Helleborus foetidus*; in addition the leaves of the cornus are variegated in summer and turn red before falling in autumn. The greenish-yellow stems of *Cornus stolonifera* 'Flaviramea' are lovely with red-leaved bergenias.

Associating flowers and foliage

Coloured foliage planted with flowers can look stunning. Simple ideas, like planting white sweet peas to climb through a purple-leaved smoke bush, can be very effective. The mango-coloured day lily 'Stella d'Oro' overtopping the reddish bronze leaves of *Heuchera* 'Chocolate Ruffles' also looks good.

OPPOSITE: Neatly clipped purple berberis surrounds artemisia and fragrant French lavender with roses behind.

Other tricks include allowing flowering plants with poor foliage to grow through foliage plants with poor flowers – planting alliums among hostas, for example. Using silver and grey foliage to soften bright reds and purples and to blend with pastel colours is a simple and almost infallible idea – just remember that most grey-leaved plants like a sunny spot that is not too wet.

Mini-themes

Having a theme for a corner, bed or border concentrates the mind wonderfully. Seasonal themes are the easiest to plan and the most likely to be colourful; you can fine-tune the colour combinations later. Colour themes are very popular but it's difficult to make them successful; the newcomer will find broader schemes – yellow and blue, purple and white, grey and pink, grey and blue – easier to make work than single colour schemes such as white, blue, yellow-and-gold, fiery shades, red flowers and foliage.

Shortcuts to good planting schemes

Here are a few tips to help you create a good scheme with effective plant associations.

- Pure white flowers will go with almost anything, although the effects they create will vary greatly according to their partners. Be careful – some 'white' flowers are actually cream or pale pink, while pure white flowers may be pink in bud or develop pinkish shades as they fade.
- Grey and silver foliage is as versatile as white flowers and of course lasts longer. It also helps to knit unlikely shades together happily.
- Creating a good background of foliage is always helpful to flowers, so a rich green hedge, a purple-leaved shrub or even a haze of tiny flowers can set off those plants in front effectively.
- Picking up similar colours in flowers and foliage usually works well – bright red flowers with red-tinted foliage, for example.
- Put broad leaves with narrow or lacy leaves.
- Make sure that borders with coloured foliage themes also have some green leaves.

Buying plants

Buying good-quality plants will get your garden off to the best possible start. This doesn't mean buying the most expensive – there are plenty of budget options available and plenty of sources.

Sourcing your plants

Buying from a garden centre or nursery is the most common source of plants, but there are a number of other good options, including the internet.

Small specialist nurseries are an excellent source for new or unusual varieties. Good advice is also often available here, but be aware that these may be small-scale operations, run by one or two busy people. Try not to take a long list of questions on a holiday weekend.

Market stalls can be good sources of common plants at competitive prices – but check the quality carefully and remember that the varieties on sale may be out of date. Never buy house plants from any outdoor stall, especially in winter. They may be severely chilled, though this may not become apparent until the next day.

Charity stalls are unpredictable as sources of plants. The first rule is not to buy sickly plants simply to support a deserving organization; there's no reason why a good plant can't be sold in a good cause. And if you give plants to a charity stall, don't use it as a way of getting rid of rubbish; they deserve better.

When you visit a garden open to the public you may well find plants on sale. This is a good way of obtaining the plants you've seen while visiting, and you may also find rare and unusual plants not on sale elsewhere.

Specialist societies organize an increasing number of plant sales, at their regular meetings and as special events. These are good places to buy both unusual and more familiar varieties and support good causes. Some of the plants on sale will demand careful cultivation, but there's usually plenty of good advice to be had. Some plant sales also have stalls run by local nurseries.

Buying from advertisements in magazines and papers can be a good source of plants, but beware of adverts that make extravagant claims and offer mixed collections of unnamed varieties – ten mixed heathers, that sort of thing. They're often the leftovers.

branches spaced evenly around a stout, straight stem. Do not buy trees growing in what looks like fresh compost, and if there are no signs of roots coming through the drainage holes, give the trunk a good pull. It may only just have been put in the pot. Check that the stem is not scraped or split and that no ties have cut into it. Make sure that the branches are not broken or dead. Buy and plant both fruit and ornamental trees in the autumn, unless you're prepared to water diligently.

Buying shrubs

Most shrubs are sold in stout plastic pots, but some evergreens and large specimens may be sold with their roots wrapped in hessian (sacking) or synthetic mesh. Shrubs sold in pots can be planted at any time of year when the soil is not waterlogged or frozen; hessian-wrapped plants should be planted in the autumn.

Roses sold in the autumn often have their bare roots wrapped in polythene, and these need planting as soon as possible. Do not buy roses with polythene-wrapped roots in spring; they will have been in the garden centre for months and may well be in poor condition. In spring, roses are usually sold in pots but are often newly potted, so, before buying, check that they're firm in their compost and that roots are peeping from the drainage holes – this is evidence that they're well established.

Do not buy shrubs that seem dry or have wilting leaves. Avoid those growing in what looks like fresh compost. Avoid shrubs with dead branches or shoots, and look out for pest or disease damage. In particular, look for plants of a good shape, with their branches spread evenly: these make the most attractive specimens.

Mail-order nurseries are good sources of unusual plants. Although you may be suspicious of buying by mail order, most nurseries offer good-quality plants and service. Many nurseries now have websites from which you can order from their full catalogue and that often list items not in their printed list. Pictures, expensive to print in catalogues, may be available online in far greater numbers. A few nurseries are online only and, generally, biggest is best – but ask around for recommendations.

Buying trees

Trees are generally sold in large pots, though you may find fruit trees sold with their roots wrapped in hessian (sacking); in some areas ornamental trees and specimen shrubs are also sold in this way. Choose a tree with its

Buying climbers

Many of the remarks set out for shrubs also apply here. It pays to buy smaller specimens whose shoots are still supple and can be trained where you need them to go rather than more mature plants with rigid branches. Small, inexpensive mail-order plants are often good value. Plants that have been set out in the nursery for some time may have twined together; carefully disentangle them or choose those that have not become entangled.

ABOVE: Unpack mail-order plants from their polythene bags as soon as they arrive and pot them up or plant them as soon as possible.

OPPOSITE: Choosing these petunias and verbenas in flower in a garden centre allows you to pick matching colours that look great together.

Buying border perennials

Perennials are usually sold in rigid plastic pots. Spring is the best time to buy; avoid those with a mass of roots growing out of the drainage holes. Avoid plants with many bare and leafless stems, but don't worry if a few leaves at the base are missing. Look for pots that are well filled, as you may be able to divide these plants into two or three pieces when planting. Avoid plants that are infected with greenfly or other pests and diseases.

Buying container and seasonal plants

Plants come either in individual pots, in packs or in strips. Pot-grown bedding plants are generally the largest, are usually in flower when you buy them, so providing an instant effect, and will usually grow away more quickly after planting. They often come in better varieties and are more expensive, but if you just need a few plants for tubs, choose pot-grown. Plants grown in strips or trays are on the whole cheaper but much smaller. They're ideal for filling in large areas. Pack-grown plants are usually in-between in size, quality and price; a pack is a series of four, six or eight small plastic pots loosely connected together.

Don't buy container or summer seasonal plants, most of which are frost-tender, until after the last frost date in your area unless you have a greenhouse or conservatory in which to protect them from late frosts. Resist buying those displayed far too early in the year, however good they look; let the nursery replace them when the freeze kills them, rather than have to replace them yourself. Avoid pest-infested plants or any with lank, wilted foliage or withered shoot tips; they may have been parched or frosted. If there's a choice, buy plants without flowers as they will usually grow away more quickly.

Plants for spring flowering are sold in bloom in late winter and spring and are also available in strips, packs and pots. You can often provide yourself with winter colour in mild areas, especially from pansies and violas, by buying them in the autumn as soon as the summer plants are over. Wallflowers are still usually grown in the open ground, rather than in pots, so they

are sold in bunches with bare roots that are kept in buckets of water. Choose plants with fresh-looking, dark green leaves.

Buying bulbs

Garden centres stock spring-flowering bulbs from late summer, and they're best planted as early in the autumn as possible. Buying bulbs that are sold loose, for you to choose yourself, enables you to pick the largest and healthiest, leaving any soft or damaged bulbs behind. Avoid buying bulbs that have been stored in obvious hot areas.

Dry snowdrops, cyclamen and winter aconite bulbs do not usually grow well, so don't buy them. Buy these in growth from specialist bulb nurseries.

Spring bulbs are also sold, in flower, in spring. This is usually a far more expensive way of buying them, but at least you can see exactly what you're getting.

Making more plants

One of the best things about gardening is that, once you have some stock, you can propagate your own plants rather than buy new ones.

Detaching young plants

The simplest way to make more plants is simply to pull a piece off the side of an existing plant in spring, a piece that already has a few roots, and plant it somewhere else. It's that easy, and if you only do it to any given plant occasionally, it works very well. It's especially successful with perennials like Michaelmas daisies, which tend to spread steadily and have shallow roots.

Beware of repeating the process too often with the same plant. The healthiest and most vigorous growth is always at the outside edge of the clump; keep taking it away and you're left with the old, unproductive growth.

Division

Division is one of the most basic methods of increasing your plant stock. You dig up the plant, split it into two or more pieces, using two forks, and replant them. Simple. Spring and autumn are the best times – choose spring if your soil is especially heavy and damp.

Many border perennials grow sufficiently quickly to be divided every three years; indeed, many suffer if not given this treatment. First cut off any old stems, then dig up the plant and rest it on the soil. Now put one fork vertically right through the middle of the clump, applying pressure if the roots are tough. Next put in your second fork in the same way, back to back with the first. Pull the two handles together, then force them apart and the clump will start to split.

Choose the most vigorous pieces from the outside of the clump to retain for planting. The woody pieces from the centre can be thrown away, though they will usually

make serviceable plants if you need them. You'll be surprised how many young plants you can obtain from one clump.

A very wide range of herbaceous perennials can be treated this way. However, some – hostas, for example – have very tough roots that may need to be cut with a spade or even an old bread knife. These, hellebores and peonies are usually better left undivided for many years.

Layering

Layering is another basic method of propagation and the one that requires least in the way of skill or tools. At its simplest, you place a rock or a brick on a branch of a shrub or climber to keep a leaf joint in contact with the soil; in time, the branch will make roots.

To achieve the very best results, however, this is how to go about it. Select a healthy shoot that is near the ground and that has grown during the earlier part of the year (not an old and woody branch). In the autumn,

ABOVE: Split large clumps of perennials by inserting two forks, back to back, and forcing them apart to break up the clump.

OPPOSITE: Protect stems of standard roses with sleeves against rabbit damage in rural areas and with insulation in very cold areas.

bend it down to the ground and excavate a depression at the point where it touches the soil. Use a hand fork to mix in some well-rotted garden compost, or used potting compost and, if the soil is heavy, some grit. Firm it well. Bend the shoot down again and peg it into the hole with a piece of forked branch or a U-shaped piece of galvanized wire (a piece of bent wire coat hanger, for example). Support the end of the shoot as it comes out from the hole by putting in a short bamboo cane and tying the shoot to it as vertically as possible. Fill the hole with a 50:50 mixture of grit and garden soil, leaving a good mound. Then make a note on the calendar for the following August and forget about it.

By late the following summer, check to see if roots have formed. Scrape away the soil on the shoot-tip side of the hole and you should find roots. If not, put back the soil, check the sturdiness of the cane and look again a few months later. If you find more than just a few roots, cut the shoot on the shrub side of the hole and leave the newly independent layer in place until the spring, when it can be transferred to its new home.

Although this is a simple method that requires almost no equipment, it takes longer than other methods to provide an independent plant – but you end up with a good-sized shrub with the minimum of effort. Climbers like clematis, Virginia creeper and wisteria, fruits like blackberries and tayberries, together with a wide variety of deciduous and evergreen shrubs, can be propagated this way. In fact it's worth trying with almost anything that produces branches sufficiently near the ground, and for magnolias it's about the only system you can rely on.

Cuttings outdoors

Taking cuttings involves cutting off a piece of a plant's stem and encouraging it to form roots. There are several methods, but that which requires the least equipment is the taking of hardwood cuttings of deciduous shrubs.

Hardwood cuttings

Hardwood cuttings are relatively long cuttings, taken in the autumn, of shoots that have ripened during the summer and autumn to become hard and woody. After leaf fall in the autumn, cut pieces about 23cm/9in long and the thickness of a pencil from the shoots that have grown during the earlier part of the year. Trim them with secateurs just below a bud at the base and just above a bud at the tip.

Choose a sheltered but not dark or shady spot outside and, if necessary, improve the soil by forking in organic matter. Then make a slit about 15cm/6in deep with your spade and put a layer of about 2.5cm/1in of grit or sharp sand in the bottom. Dip the cuttings in hormone rooting powder, then stand them about 7.5cm/3in apart in the slit with the base of each resting on the sand. Finally, close the slit by firming with your boot. Label the row and then simply leave them.

Most, if not all, should start to grow in the spring, but they're best left to continue growing until the autumn, a year after they were put in, when they can be moved to their permanent sites.

Plants that root well using this method include roses (especially climbers and ramblers), willows and poplars, buddleias, blackcurrants, elder, cotoneaster, jasmine and philadelphus, plus a wide range of other deciduous shrubs and also some trees like laburnum. Cuttings of

many evergreen shrubs can be taken at the same time of year, but usually require the protection of a cold frame or cold greenhouse.

Cuttings indoors

Cuttings of many plants can also be taken indoors; these require more equipment and more attention. They're usually taken in spring and summer from new leafy shoot tips, and may be quite soft if taken in the early part of the season or from indoor plants. Alternatively they may be 'semi-ripe'; that is, the tips may still be soft but 2.5–5cm/1–2in farther down the shoot they will have started to harden.

ABOVE: Use sharp secateurs to take a cutting from the tip of a healthy shoot. Make sure the cutting is quickly stored in polythene or potted to prevent it drying out.

OPPOSITE: Water seedlings with a rose on the watering can to create a fine spray, but be sure not to overwater as this will encourage disease.

Soft and semi-ripe cuttings

Soft cuttings are taken from new spring shoots of shrubs and some perennials and summer seasonal plants; they're more delicate and less easy to look after. Semi-ripe cuttings of shrubs are taken in the second half of the summer and are slightly tougher.

Use sharp secateurs to take 10–12.5cm/4–5in cuttings from the tips of healthy shoots, putting them into polythene bags to prevent them from drying out. Cuttings from perennials and container plants like busy lizzies can be a little shorter. Trim the cuttings to just below a leaf joint, reducing the length to about 7.5cm/3in. This can be done using sharp secateurs; soft shoots can often be trimmed with kitchen scissors. Remove the leaves on the lower half of the cuttings carefully.

Plants that root very easily, like begonias, impatiens, ivies and African violets, can be rooted in water. Cover a jam jar with a piece of kitchen foil, then make a series of small nicks in it with the point of a kitchen knife. Remove the foil, fill the jar with water, replace the foil and push the base of the cuttings through the holes into the water so that the foil holds them in place. Stand the jar on a warm windowsill and roots will soon form. The roots formed in this way are often rather brittle, so it pays to move the rooted cuttings into pots while the roots are still short, about 12mm/½in.

Most cuttings should be placed in pots of fresh, moist seed or multipurpose compost. A 7.5cm/3in pot will take from three to eight cuttings, depending on the spread of their leaves. Loosely fill with compost level with the rim, tap the base of the pot on the table to settle it, then use a pencil or dibber to make a hole in the compost. Firm each cutting in gently, water the pot and label it.

Stand each pot in a clear polythene bag, then lift the bag up around the cuttings and tie it at the top. This creates a humid atmosphere that prevents the cuttings from wilting. Place the pot on a windowsill or in a conservatory out of direct light. Direct sunlight will heat up the inside of the bag and damage the soft leaves.

If you plan to take more than just a few cuttings, it's a good idea to invest in a thermostatically controlled heated propagator that will help rooting by keeping the base of the cuttings warmer than the tip. Models are available that are designed to fit on a windowsill

Rooting of some plants can take as little as a few days, while others may take a few weeks. It's important that the cuttings never dry out in this time. You can tell when they've rooted, as they'll start to grow; if a gentle pull on the cutting reveals resistance, you can be sure that rooting has begun. Roots will eventually appear at the drainage holes in the bottom of the pots.

Plants suitable for this treatment include many shrubs (these are best rooted from semi-ripe cuttings), house plants (soft cuttings of tradescantia, for example, are produced all the year round) and border perennials (choose new spring shoots from the base).

Aftercare

When rooted, the cuttings can be potted up individually. Knock the cuttings out of their pot by upturning the pot and tapping the rim on the edge of a table or worktop. Gently pull the rooted cuttings apart and pot them up carefully. They will need to be cosseted a little, perhaps kept in an unheated propagator, for a few days, until they start to grow again, when they can look after themselves.

Seeds

Growing from seed is another way to fill your garden with plants, and is a particularly suitable propagation method for many flowering plants and vegetables.

Buying seeds

A limited range of seed is available in chain stores and DIY stores, more in garden centres and a much wider range by mail order. Most seed companies state the number of seeds contained in their packets and this makes it easier to ensure you get good value.

The time to buy seeds in garden centres is in late winter and spring, when the racks have been newly

stocked. I would not suggest buying in the autumn, not even varieties for autumn sowing, as they will have been exposed to the heat and possibly damp of the garden centre for many months by this time. If the seeds are not sown within a few weeks of buying them, seal the packets in a polythene bag and leave them in the bottom of the fridge until sowing time.

Buying seeds by mail order gives you a much wider selection to choose from. The seed catalogues are all free and appear in the autumn; many seed companies now have their seed catalogues online and you can order direct from the website. As well as listing and illustrating the varieties available, catalogues also provide much useful information on the plants and how to grow them. Some of the mail-order companies also produce leaflets or booklets giving guidance on how to grow their seeds successfully.

As well as seeds, catalogues often list seedlings and young plants of some varieties, especially those that are difficult to germinate. These can be invaluable if you like to bring plants on but are without the facilities, time, experience or inclination to start them from seed.

Seedlings and young plants can also be useful if you wish to grow seeds like begonias, which can be tricky to grow well. If you order seedlings or young plants, you'll receive them after the most difficult germination stage is over.

Sowing seeds

Sowing seeds outside is the simplest method of growing plants from seed and is used for hardy annuals and biennials, some hardy perennials and most vegetables. This method suits all hardy annuals, the tougher half-hardy annuals, biennials and those perennials easily raised from seed. Most vegetables are also raised in this way. Check the advice on your seed packets. While a wide range of plants can be raised by sowing in the open garden, should there be space, others need extra warmth and protection.

In a small garden there may not be much choice over where you sow your seeds. Most, except biennials and some vegetables, are sown where they are to grow, while the rest are raised in a seed bed and then transplanted to their final sites. Here's how to go about it. The seed packet will give advice on when to sow – always read the advice on the packet before starting and follow it, as it will be more specific than the advice I can give here.

Let's take as an example: some lettuce for your vegetable bed. You'll need scissors, a border fork, a rake, your measuring rod, some fertilizer and maybe some garden compost. Remove any weeds from the site, then fork over the site to the depth of the fork; if the soil is poor, add a bucketful, or perhaps a little more, of well-rotted compost per square metre/yard and fork it in.

RIGHT: Some varieties of perennials, like this poppy 'Pizzicato', will flower in the first summer after sowing the seed in spring.

OPPOSITE: This mock orange can be increased by taking short cuttings in late summer that will soon root.

Tread it, rake it level, then rake in a handful of balanced general fertilizer to each square metre/yard.

Check the instructions on the packet to see how far apart to sow the seed – they often suggest rows 23cm/9in apart. With your measuring rod as a straight edge, use a piece of stick, or even your index finger, to make a groove in the soil (known as a drill) about 12mm/½in deep, or as directed on the packet.

Cut the top off the seed packet with a pair of scissors and then, if there's a smaller pack inside, cut the top off that too. Make a crease halfway along one edge of the cut top and then hold the sides of the packet between thumb and middle finger. Holding the crease low over the end of the drill, tilt the packet slightly and tap it with the index finger; this will encourage seeds to roll down the crease and drop off into the soil. You'll be able to watch them as they fall and make sure they're sown evenly as you move the packet along the length of the drill. Lettuce seeds, which usually germinate well and make large plants, can usefully go in about 2.5cm/1in apart. Seeds of smaller plants should be sown more closely.

When the seeds have been sown, mark the ends of the rows with small pieces of twig or canes, then cover the seeds. This is done by standing upright and using the back of the rake to draw a little soil from alongside the drill over the seeds. Then use the flat of the rake to tamp them gently into place. Finally, put in a label naming the variety you have sown and the date.

Hardy annuals, biennials and perennials are sown in just the same way, and other vegetables too.

Thinning out

When the seeds come up, check the instructions on the packet to find the final spacing, as the seedlings will need thinning out (removing surplus seedlings). Seedlings from this second stage of thinning can be transplanted elsewhere.

ABOVE: After seedlings have come through, progressively remove the weaker ones to leave the plants at their proper final spacing.

OPPOSITE: Collect your own seeds from foxgloves and sow in a pot or a spare piece of ground to produce plenty of plants for the following year.

The simplest way to thin seedlings is to place the first and second fingers of one hand closely on either side of the seedling you wish to retain, and pull out those seedlings that are surplus. Larger seedlings for transplanting need more careful removal with a trowel. Watering the rows first helps the seedlings to cope with any disturbance.

Transplanting

Biennials and perennials must be transplanted to a wider spacing to give them room to grow. Again, check the packet for precise instructions, as the spacing depends on the variety concerned. Transplanting is usually done after the seedlings have been thinned out once.

First water the row well and then, using a trowel, carefully lift the seedlings, keeping as much soil as you can on the roots of each. Place them in a box and cover the roots with soil to prevent them from drying out. Set out your garden line on the new site, and plant them at the required spacing, using your measuring rod as a guide. Water them in thoroughly.

This method suits all hardy annuals, the tougher half-hardy annuals, biennials and those perennials that are easily raised from seed. Most vegetables are also raised in this way. Again, check the advice on your seed packets.

Collecting and storing seed

Many plants in the garden produce seed. Some, like poppies and love-lies-bleeding, scatter prodigious quantities, so it seems obvious that this seed could be collected and sown. But it's not that simple. Many of the plants we grow, especially bedding plants like petunias, marigolds and geraniums, are complicated hybrids and when the seed they produce is sown, the resulting plants may be nothing like their parents.

Try it by all means. Plants grown from seed of some plants that are actually wild species, like poached egg plants and baby blue eyes, should be exactly the same as their parents, but be prepared for a few surprises among roses, chrysanthemums, dahlias and anything listed in a seed catalogue as an F1 hybrid.

Chapter 7

Vegetables and Fruits

Growing your own produce can give you a great sense of achievement as well as provide delicious things to eat. Newcomers to growing food do not always realize that choosing a good variety really does make a difference. Simply picking a vegetable seed packet off the rack because the picture looks appealing can be a mistake. Mail-order catalogues offer the best selection, and the seed packets always provide advice on how to sow the seed. Fruit trees and bushes must also be chosen carefully if you are to achieve a good crop.

Growing vegetables

Finding space for vegetables in a small garden is often a problem, as most of us like the garden to look attractive for as much of the year as possible and vegetables are not seen as contributing to the aesthetics of the outdoor space. At the same time, however, there really is nothing quite like eating food you've grown yourself just minutes after it's been picked. Even after years of badgering, supermarkets still offer too much tasteless pulp. So grow your own vegetables: it's not difficult, they don't necessarily take up much space – and vegetables can look good too.

Planting systems

The traditional system of growing vegetables is probably the least appropriate for a small garden. The system consists of dividing an area into three parts, and dividing the crops into three groups. Each area receives different pre-season treatment. Crops rotate around the three plots year by year, giving a three-year cycle of crop-growing and preparation. To make the traditional system work well, you need so much space that you probably wouldn't have any room left for growing flowers.

Most productive, for the small garden and the large garden alike, is the bed system, especially when coupled with other modern techniques. The deep bed system involves preparing a 1.2m/4ft wide bed by double digging and growing the crops in short rows across the bed. The rich, deep, loose soil encourages plant roots to penetrate farther than normal and so have access to greater reserves of moisture and plant foods. Combine this with tighter than usual spacing and you can get an astonishing yield from a small space.

Although it's unusual to organize a traditional crop rotation system for deep beds, it's also unusual for the pest and disease problems associated with a lack of rotation to cause problems. This is because walking on the beds is prohibited, so soil-borne diseases are less likely to be transferred from one bed to another – as long as you clean your tools properly.

A simpler version involves using a bed system but preparing less deeply (which is, after all, hard work). This has all the benefits of accessibility, adaptability and much of the productivity but without the strenuous preparation.

The potager is a vegetable garden that is, in itself, ornamental. In its contemporary incarnation it usually consists of an attractive arrangement of beds edged with dwarf shrubs such as box, lavender or hyssop. The beds themselves may each hold just one crop or may be subdivided by rows of crop plants to create an attractive pattern. They may be themed for summer or winter, can include rows of cut flowers and plantings of edible flowers and, thoughtfully planned, will combine beauty, productivity and flavour in one design.

Containers can also be used to grow a little food in the smallest of spaces, and with the use of special patio varieties and those with ornamental features this can be a very attractive and productive option.

Integrating vegetables and flowers

Any small garden vegetable planting is enhanced by using vegetables that are themselves attractive enough for the flower border: red cabbage, runner beans, red lettuce, purple kale, the many-coloured chards. And in small spaces this is another way to go: integrating flowers and vegetables completely, using them as the valuable foliage and flowering plants they are. Planting purple cabbages with silvery artemisia or white chard with scarlet Million Bells brings a new look to ornamental borders.

But, inevitably, when you grow vegetables as ornamentals, compromise is in the air. When your curly red lettuce is ready to pick, looking so good in front of that white-edged hosta, do you cut it, ruin the display

OPPOSITE: Combining a quick crop of cabbages with growing variegated irises on to a large size before planting in the border creates an unusual and attractive display in a limited space.

and leave a gaping hole? Or do you leave it until it runs to seed in a steeple of frilly red leaves? Do you sacrifice the lunch or the look?

Vegetables in borders

In a small space, the most exciting way to grow vegetables is to integrate them into the borders with the shrubs, climbers, perennials and annuals. The vegetables you choose must be attractive both in form and colour, and often this means choosing very specific varieties: after all, some lettuces are dramatic or intriguing foliage plants while others are little more than green blobs. However, the varieties of vegetables you need may only be available as seed, not plants, and you will need to grow them yourself.

Ornamental herbs are mostly shrubs and perennials and integrate far more easily: coloured-leaved sages and thymes would be grown as ornamentals if they had no other value.

Planting ideas for borders

Use shapes and colours as the basis for your plant associations. Here are a few ideas:
• Train runner beans or purple-podded peas on canes as a feature in the border.
• Plant runner beans or purple-podded peas under mature spring flowering shrubs like forsythia to add summer colour.
• Interplant blue-leaved hostas and purple-podded French beans.
• Back variegated hostas with curly red kale.
• Set globe artichokes or cardoons at the back of the border with purple foliage in front.
• Interplant black kale with blue petunias.
• Grow dwarf rusty marigolds among red lettuce.

The potager

A potager is an ornamental vegetable and herb garden, usually with a basis of permanent planting. The versions

OPPOSITE: Who said vegetables are dull? Kales, sage and purple-leaved fennel with flowering persicaria provide a long-lasting colour-themed feature.

now seen are generally less formal in layout, and more relaxed in style (not to say smaller), than the huge and famous potager at Villandry in France. The beds are usually regular in shape, and are edged with low hedging in box, santolina, hyssop or lavender, or sometimes with a less permanent crop such as curled parsley or even cottage pinks.

The paths are best gravelled or laid in bricks, and the beds themselves may be planted with just one crop or may be divided into sections by rows of neat plants, such as the bushy, variegated nasturtium 'Alaska' or chives. Each section is then planted with an individual crop.

Try to provide the potager with as much sun as possible, although summer shade is valuable in climates with hot summers. Digging and incorporating organic matter into the potager is the way to start, creating a rich and fertile soil that will support a continuous succession of cropping.

Plants for your potager

A small potager can be used for the more unusual and attractive salads, herbs, edible flowers and garnishes. You could try any of the following:
• balm (yellow-leaved lemon balm)
• basil (green- and purple-leaved)
• calendulas
• chervil
• chives
• fennel 'Smokey' (purple-leaved type)
• feverfew (yellow-leaved)
• hyssop
• land cress
• marjoram (golden-leaved)
• mint (variegated ginger mint and variegated apple mint)
• nasturtium 'Alaska'
• parsley (curled and French)
• par-cel (celery-flavoured parsley)
• sage (coloured-leaved types)
• thyme (bushy types, ordinary and lemon)
• violets

Deep beds

The deep bed system is the most productive system for serious vegetable growers; a huge amount can be grown in a small space. It is ideal for small gardens, as it can be adapted to fit whatever space is available. It also enables you to grow the maximum yield from the minimum of space.

A deep bed consists of a bed about 1.2m/4ft wide and as long as you care to make it. Rows run across the bed, so they are short, and it's therefore easy to grow small quantities for a small household. By sowing a number of short rows over a period it's easier to avoid the glut of produce that so often results from sowing one long row. You will also enjoy the easy access from the paths, making harvesting in all weathers simple. Mulch the paths alongside the beds and you can pick peas in your slippers.

Deep beds are suitable for all crops except sprouts (which are generally a waste of space in small gardens anyway, although purple-leaved forms make superb foliage plants for the border). A deep bed will also tend to ensure that you do not produce the familiar surfeit of runner beans. Try just one row, across the bed, and see if this produces enough.

Siting

Deep beds should be sited in an open, sunny spot. Shelter from wind is helpful, but if possible the beds should receive sunshine all day. The next best option is a site partially shaded by a fence or wall. Avoid making deep beds under trees; crops will be poor. If you're making more than one deep bed, allow a path of about 60cm/2ft between the beds.

If you like a neat, crisp finish to your beds, they can be edged with vertical boards to keep the soil in place. Use 15 x 2.5cm/6 x 1in pressure-treated boards held in place by screwing them with 4cm/1½in brass screws, countersunk to 5 x 2.5cm/2 x 1in pressure-treated posts

(on the inside). The boards can be stained to a colour that suits your garden and setting, and the path between can be mulched with gravel or bark. Laying landscape fabric underneath the mulch will prevent almost all weed growth.

ABOVE: Basil, chives, thymes and other herbs will thrive in a sunny corner and require very little space to make an attractive and useful planting.

OPPOSITE: Climbing vegetables like cucumbers and squashes can be trained on a timber fence, which will need to be stout to take the weight.

Preparation

Ideally, each bed should be double dug, incorporating organic matter (see page 99). Rather than leaving the organic matter in a layer at the base of the trench as is sometimes recommended, it's important to fork it into both the lower and the upper layer to create a good mix and so spread its water-holding capacity and its nutrients evenly through the depth of soil into which roots will penetrate. Spread 5cm/2in on the lower spit before forking that over, followed by 5cm/2in on the surface, then fork that in. Do not tread on the soil at all after it has been dug.

The loosening of the soil and the addition of organic matter will raise the level of the bed considerably above the surrounding soil level. Apart from tidying the edges it should be left alone. It will sink, of course, but if it has been dug evenly, it will sink evenly. Extra fertilizer is raked in between crops, but beds are not dug again for three years, after which they are completely remade with another generous application of organic matter.

General cultivation

Crops are grown in short rows running across the bed. Plants are grown closer together than usual, to make the most of the available space. You can sow quick-maturing crops like radishes in between the rows. Sowing and planting are done without treading on the bed and with the minimum of firming. Weeds can be removed by hand or hoed off easily, but regular mulching with weed-free organic matter will help to conserve moisture, prevent rain from washing the soil on to the path and improve the soil.

Watering is best carried out using seephose (rather than a wasteful sprinkler), which can be laid along the bed and covered with mulch.

Early crops

Forcing a few early crops is easy in deep beds, as cloches are available that cover the whole bed to a length of 1.2m/4ft, and if a variety of crops are grown side by side under just one or two cloches, they can all be forced together.

Basic beds

Preparing deep beds to double the depth of the digging spade can be a real chore, so many gardeners use a simpler bed system. The beds are marked out in the same way but are only cultivated to a depth of about 25–30cm/10–12in (rather than 45–50cm/18–20in). This can be done by digging with a fork and mixing in friable weed-free organic matter or, even simpler, by hiring a rotary cultivator.

Make one or two passes with the rotary cultivator to loosen the soil, spread 7.5cm/3in of organic matter on the surface, then make a final pass to mix it in. A little raking may be needed to even out the levels. Even simpler, cultivate to a depth of about 23cm/9in, then remove the top few centimetres or inches from the path and spread this on the surface of the bed before working in organic matter. Sow and plant across the bed, mulch to suppress weeds and improve the soil, and use seephose for watering.

Containers

Using containers can often provide the only opportunity to grow a little food in a very small garden or where there is no suitable place for a vegetable plot.

Choosing

Vegetables need moisture and nutrients, and the simplest way to provide them is by using large containers where the bulk of compost will help to provide reservoirs of both. Large tubs, the biggest you can find, are ideal. Move them into a sunny position and set them on blocks or pot feet (for drainage) before filling. A large tub is ideal for tomatoes or peppers, or even climbing beans, which can be surrounded by smaller crops.

Large window boxes can be used for smaller quick-growing crops like lettuce, radish and spring onion, and for herbs such as parsley, as long as you water regularly. You can even grow tomatoes and peppers in hanging baskets if you choose varieties that have a trailing habit. You will need to water and feed them well.

Growing bags – large rectangular plastic bags filled with compost – are intended for tomatoes but are also suitable for peppers, aubergines, climbing beans, lettuce, chard and even round carrots and baby turnips. The only problem is that growing bags are not very attractive; however, containers designed to hide them are becoming available. Or you can plant clouds of blue lobelia around the edges to trail down and cover the plastic.

Compost

Growing bags come ready-filled, but other containers need to be filled with fresh multipurpose or potting compost from the garden centre; do not use old compost or garden soil.

Crops

Tomatoes are the classic container crop, but peppers, aubergines and bush cucumbers will also thrive. Climbing beans, lettuce, round carrots, baby turnips, radishes, spring onions and chard also do well, as do

many herbs. Parsley is the classic container herb, and although the curly types are less flavoursome than plain-leaved parsley, they look better. Basil does well in areas with warm nights.

Maintenance

There are two crucial aspects to looking after vegetables in containers: watering and feeding. Keep these in mind before you buy your pots. As they mature, tomatoes in growing bags will need watering every single day and sometimes twice a day. If you think this is going to be a problem, consider larger containers – though even large tubs will often need watering every day if they're supporting tomatoes, chard or other thirsty crops. A drip watering system is ideal, but at least be sure to install an outside tap so you can water using a hosepipe.

Regular feeding is important too. The only type you'll need is a liquid tomato feed, which can be applied to all your vegetable crops every week.

Vegetable crops

The most practical crops to grow in small gardens are those that give a particularly good yield from a small space, provide good-quality produce that may be difficult to find or unreasonably expensive in the shops and are at their best when very fresh. When space is limited, the last thing you want to do is grow crops that take up a vast amount of room for a small yield of produce that is available in the shops anyway.

Aubergines

Tall varieties of this fruiting and flowering vegetable need hot summers to thrive outside, but dwarf patio types grown in pots are more adaptable. Different cultivars produce different colours: dark purple, yellowish-green or white.

Dwarf or French beans

These are often expensive and of moderate quality in the shops, and frequently imported from far away. Choose those with yellow, purple or speckled pods held above the foliage where their colour is visible.

Runner beans

The familiar runner bean is easy to grow. Runner beans are so prolific that it's best to grow only one wigwam, or one short row, especially if you are growing other beans too. Choose those few varieties with especially attractive flowers.

Early carrots

Quick-maturing, finger-sized or round carrots make an invaluable small garden crop that can mature throughout the summer – and the foliage is pretty too.

LEFT: A terracotta strawberry pot can be used for growing many crops; here, summer salads are getting established.

OPPOSITE: Tomatoes grow well in containers of all kinds. Choose something stylish like this galvanized planter to bring a little panache to the planting.

and it hides the fruits. Courgettes can be grown in pots but need generous watering.

Cucumbers

Bush cucumbers can be very successful when grown outside, and they are very tasty too. They can even be grown in pots.

Cut-and-come-again crops

This is an approach to growing salads that requires very little space and produces a quick crop, so it's ideal for a garden with a limited amount of space. Basically, this is what you get in the pre-packed bags of spring salad mix (sometimes called mesclun) at the supermarket. The leaves are cut as required, left to regrow, then cut again, sometimes a second or third time. Suitable crops include rocket, lettuce, cress, endive, pak choi, mizuna and chard, or you can buy a seed mixture.

Endive

Endives are an increasingly popular salad vegetable. The frilly, cut-leaved types are especially useful and also the most attractive.

Lettuces

There are four types of lettuce and all are worth growing in the small garden.

Cabbage lettuce (sometimes called soft or butterhead lettuce) has a soft-leaved head with dark green outer leaves and a paler heart.

Crisp lettuce has a crisp heart and crinkled foliage. Iceberg lettuce (crisp lettuce with the outer leaves removed) is large and very dense and there are a few red-leaved varieties.

Cos lettuce is an upright lettuce, distinguished by its long, narrow leaves and distinctive flavour. There are some attractive speckled and red-leaved types.

Chard

The most colourful of vegetables, chards can be cropped all season by pulling off the outer leaves and in many areas will overwinter to provide a crop in the spring too. Those with brightly coloured stems are pretty enough to be grown in the flower border.

Courgettes

These large, spreading plants produce small, tasty fruits (if harvested regularly) all summer. Even the bush types, rather than old-fashioned trailing ones, hog space. Some think the bold foliage is attractive, but it's often spiny

ABOVE: These 'Painted Lady' runner beans, with their bicoloured red and white flowers, provide decoration long before the beans are ready.

OPPOSITE: Even onions and leeks can bring bold structure, as well as colour, to the vegetable garden with their strong habit and blue foliage.

Loose-leaf lettuce do not develop a dense head but instead produce a constant supply of foliage on a loose plant. Most of the attractive varieties come into this category.

Leeks

This valuable and delicious winter vegetable is striking when covered in frost.

Parsnips

Parsnips are a long-season crop that grows particularly well in deep beds. Frost can actually improve the flavour of this hardy vegetable.

Peas

Mangetout, tall purple-podded, and leafless peas are the best value in small gardens. Mangetout produce by far the best crop from a given area of ground. Purple-podded peas (which also have purple flowers) are certainly the most decorative, and leafless peas are entirely self-supporting, which is very useful when growing vegetables in beds.

Peppers

Both sweet peppers and chilli peppers have a place in the small garden. Patio types are especially suited to containers, mixed borders and potagers.

Radicchio

Green and loose-leaved in summer, the leaves redden in autumn and form hearts. Radicchio is good for winter colour and attractive with early spring bulbs.

Radishes

An ideal small garden crop, radishes mature so quickly that they can be easily fitted in among other crops in any sunny place.

Spring onions

This quick-growing salad crop can be grown in small patches, window boxes and growing bags.

Tomatoes

All three types of tomato plant are a valuable crop for small gardens.

Modern bush varieties Ideal for beds, producing a good crop in most parts of the country.

Tall types Can be grown across deep beds or in groups of three in the border.

Patio tomatoes Dwarf and trailing types for tubs and baskets.

Turnips

Grow turnips in your garden as a quick summer crop, not for storage.

Growing fruit

Until recently, growing fruit in a small garden would have been a problem because almost everything available was so big, but techniques and varieties have been improved, and now anyone can grow fruit in a small space.

Improvements and innovations

A number of innovations have made it possible to grow more and more luscious fruit in smaller and smaller spaces.

- Dwarf trees and new ways of training them have enabled tree fruits to be grown in small spaces and even in pots.
- Disease-resistant varieties have reduced the need for spraying.
- The removal of virus diseases from planting stock has greatly increased productivity, so you need far fewer plants to get a good crop.
- Completely new, heavy-cropping fruits like the tayberry (a raspberry/blackberry hybrid) have been created.
- New pruning techniques have been developed to enable gardeners to get large crops from small trees.
- Varieties have been developed that extend the cropping period at the beginning or the end of the season.

Integrating fruit into the garden

Some crops, such as small-scale apples and cherries, cordon and fan-shaped trees, cane fruits and alpine strawberries, can be happily integrated into the rest of the garden. Most smaller fruit can be easily grown with vegetables as well.

Almost all fruit requires plenty of sun to produce the most blossom and the largest, tastiest crop. Bearing that in mind, here are some ways in which fruit and ornamental plants can be used together.

- Espaliered apples can be trained on the fence at the back of the border; plants in front should not shade them too much.
- Small apple trees and cherries can be used as in-border specimens and focal points.
- Raspberries can be trained up a single post as a feature in the border and intertwined with clematis.
- Blackberries and tayberries can be trained on wires at the back of the border.
- Apples, blackberries and tayberries can support annual climbers like canary creeper and sweet peas (but not nasturtiums, which are too smothering).
- Pot-grown apples, cherries, peaches, apricots and nectarines can be sited on a sunny patio.
- Alpine strawberries can be used as ground-covering clumps in partially shaded borders and under mature deciduous shrubs.

Planting fruit

Most fruit, with the exception of strawberries, is planted in the autumn. Tree fruits are planted in the same way as other trees, bush fruits like deciduous shrubs and strawberries and rhubarb like perennials. (See page 102 for more detail about planting.)

Siting

Generally speaking, fruit needs an open, sunny situation with shelter from the wind. Shelter is especially important in spring, when biting winds can deter vital pollinating insects. Frost also needs considering, and planting fruit in a frost pocket will increase the likelihood of damage to blossoms, ruining the crops.

Soil improvement

Ideally, the soil for fruit needs to be fairly rich and well drained. The requirements of different fruits vary, but in most gardens it's perfectly possible to grow a wide range of types, although sometimes careful selection of varieties will be necessary. Suitable soil can generally be created from almost any basic material, although in waterlogged soil it's not usually possible to grow good fruit.

OPPOSITE: Cane fruits like these raspberries are ideal for small gardens as the regular pruning they require helps to keep them neat.

You can improve soil fertility by adding liberal quantities of organic matter to dry, sandy soil and to heavy clay and then mulching regularly.

The fruit cage

It pays to gather as much of your fruit as you can together in one spot and protect it from marauding birds with netting. The fruit cage is simply a netting structure supported on steel poles that keeps the birds off the crop. Fruit cages come in easy-to-build kit form and can be supplied in a size to fit your plot exactly. A fruit cage can be a good idea even in a small garden, especially if you make the most of the protected space by moving salad crops or cut flowers inside.

Feeding

For most fruits, feeding consists of applying a dressing of fertilizer in the spring, immediately followed by mulching the plants with organic matter to keep down weeds. The mulch will also improve long-term fertility and provide a long, steady supply of plant foods to encourage a good crop of fruit.

Pruning

Techniques vary considerably from crop to crop, but it's important to remember that pruning is vital in a small garden. Not only will pruning restrict the size of your trees and bushes to manageable proportions, but it will also ensure that you pick the heaviest possible crop from your plants.

ABOVE: Crab apples are ideal pollinators for all apple trees and also produce these attractive, and useful, autumn fruits.
OPPOSITE: It is possible to get a good crop of fruit even in a small garden. By training apples carefully and pruning them regularly, it's not difficult to produce a large crop from just a single tree.

Tree fruit

A big old apple tree that fruits badly is a depressing but all too common feature of a small garden attached to an older property. Now new techniques and varieties enable almost all fruits to be grown on productive small trees that fit a small space.

Apples

Apples can be generous croppers in a small garden, and by making a few thoughtful choices at the start, you can make life easy for yourself and your trees. Apples will grow on most soils and in most situations, although they're often unhappy on shallow soil over solid chalk, in salty winds, in very heavy rainfall, in the shade and some are unhappy at high altitudes. So, in effect, the vast majority of gardens will grow apples well, but you may need to choose your variety and rootstock carefully.

Apple trees for small gardens

An apple tree is made up of two parts. Almost all of the above-ground part of the tree is the variety by which it is usually known – 'Cox's Orange Pippin', 'Spartan', etc. The below-ground rootstock, to which it is grafted, governs the eventual size of the tree. There are six types of apple tree that are appropriate for the small garden.

Cordons: A tree restricted to a single main stem, trained at an angle of 45° on a fence or on wires and restricted to about 1.8m/6ft in height. Fruit is carried close to the main stem. Easy and productive, this is the top choice for small gardens.

Espaliers: A single vertical stem carries a series of parallel horizontal tiers tied to wires on each side. Although a mature espalier is very elegant and attractive, espaliers are expensive to buy and training is more difficult than for a cordon.

Bush trees: Exactly what the name implies: a bushy tree on a short trunk, but grown on a rootstock that keeps it to no more than 1.8–2.4m/6–8ft high. Bush

trees are easy to maintain but need regular pruning to crop well, and although relatively small can still take up too much space. Bush trees can be grown in large pots, making a valuable patio feature.

Step-overs: Two branches, trained at 180° to each other, 30cm/12in above the ground. Step-over trees are used as edging to flowerbeds or potagers, the branches running parallel to the path. They provide a productive change from box edging, but must be pruned on hands and knees and can be a tripping hazard.

Columnar trees: There are two ways of creating apple trees in a very narrow, columnar shape. The Ballerina

Series is a limited range of varieties specially bred to grow this way, naturally, without pruning. They reach about 2.4m/8ft after five years but continue to grow. They need no pruning, but the fruit quality is suspect and they can be disease prone.

Minarette trees: These are the more familiar varieties grown as a single vertical stem trained and pruned like a cordon. Although the fruit is better quality, they need regular pruning, which can be difficult on tall, mature specimens. They make excellent exclamation marks at the corners of a formal garden.

Rootstocks

When you buy a tree the rootstock will always be named alongside the variety itself.

M27: This rootstock produces a very dwarf tree and is the best choice for trees to be grown in pots. In the garden, a bush tree should reach about 1.8m/6ft in height after fifteen years.

M9: This is a slightly less dwarfing rootstock, and is the best all-round choice in a small garden where the soil is good. It is suitable for both small bush trees, which eventually reach 2.1–2.4m/7–8ft in height, and for cordons.

M26: Being similar to M9 rootstock but a little more vigorous, M26 is the best choice for a small garden that has poor soil. On good soil it will produce a taller bush.

MM106: This is an altogether less dwarfing rootstock, making substantial bushy trees, and is not suitable for the smallest gardens or for cordons. Most trees are grown on this stock, and it is the one most widely available in garden centres.

MM111 and **M2:** These rootstocks produce large trees that are unsuitable for small gardens.

Soil and situation

Apples will grow on most soils and in most situations although they're often unhappy on shallow soil over solid chalk, in salty winds, in very heavy rainfall, in the shade and some are unhappy at high altitudes. So, in effect, the vast majority of gardens will grow apples well, but you may need to choose your variety and rootstock carefully.

Pollination

Pollination can seem tricky for newcomers to fruit growing, but it's really not a problem. The flowers of most apple varieties must receive pollen from a different apple variety to ensure that they produce a good crop of fruits. Different varieties flower at different periods in the spring, so to enable the bees to take pollen from one tree to another, the flowering period of trees intended to pollinate each other must overlap, at least partially.

The simplest small garden option, especially if you only have space for one tree, is to plant one of the few self-fertile apples, which require no other tree to provide pollen. The choice is limited: 'Goldilocks', 'Greensleeves' and 'Queen Cox' are the best.

Crab apples

For crab apple jelly, the variety 'John Downie' is the best. It makes an erect tree with white flowers followed by large orange fruits, and it will also pollinate eating and culinary apples. Other varieties are 'Golden Hornet', with its long season of flowering followed by large golden fruit, 'Aldenhamensis', 'Hillieri' and 'Wintergold'.

Pears

Pears are altogether less easy to deal with in small gardens than apples. Although looked after in much the same way, they're more trouble and less reliable – though people who are allergic to apples can usually eat them. There are no widely available rootstocks to keep the trees small.

I would not recommend growing pears in a small space. If you really must have a pear, grow 'Duodena' on Quince C rootstock and train it on a wall.

OPPOSITE: A pear, trained on a wall, not only looks attractive but can be amazingly productive, although it is more difficult to grow than an apple tree. Always buy a tree on which the nursery has begun the training.

Stone fruits

Stone fruits can be grown in small spaces if you choose the right variety. They are generally grown in bush or fan form.

Cherries

The introduction of self-fertile sweet cherry varieties that do not need a second variety as pollinator, together with dwarfing rootstocks, has made it possible to grow cherries in a relatively confined space. Sweet cherries are grown either as bushes or, in colder areas where they do not always thrive in the open, as fans on a wall.

Plums

Plums, damsons and greengages can all be dealt with together. Plums…we all know. Damsons are smaller than plums and usually have a rather astringent flavour; greengages are also smaller than plums, and especially sweet and scented, but need good growing conditions to thrive.

Peaches and nectarines

Picking a peach or nectarine fresh from your own garden may be something to boast about to the neighbours, but in many areas producing a good crop is not easy. In areas with cold winters and especially hot summers, trees can be grown in the open garden. In areas with cooler summers, you need a warm, sunny wall – facing south or south-west. Naturally dwarf varieties suitable for containers are now becoming available.

Both peaches and nectarines are self-fertile, but in areas with relatively warm winters they will flower early in the year, when few bees are around, so they may need help from artificial pollination, using a cotton bud or a child's paintbrush.

LEFT: Plums can be so productive that the mass of fruit weighs down the branches. On small trees it is especially important to thin out the fruit before branches break.

OPPOSITE: Strawberries are among the best fruits for small gardens as they crop well from a small space.

Apricots

In many ways apricots are treated in much the same way as peaches, so it can be assumed that they need the same cultivation, with the following exceptions.

Apricots have a definite preference for a well-drained, limy soil, and like nothing better than a good loam over limestone – though any well-drained limy soil will do. They especially appreciate the addition of plenty of organic matter. Naturally dwarf varieties suitable for containers are now becoming available.

Grapes

Grapes can be grown in a warm, sheltered, preferably south-west facing spot in the open, or can be trained on a south- or south-west facing wall or fence. In warm areas grapes can be grown in more open situations, but they will not thrive in areas that have cool, dull summers.

On a fence or wall, grapevines should be trained to wires on a cordon system – though they're more often left to ramble, in which case they take up huge amounts of space and fruit poorly. When grown in the open they're trained on wires, and a system of renewal pruning known as the Guyot system is adopted. All grapes are self-fertile, so they pose no pollination problems.

Berries

Raspberries, loganberries, blackberries and a number of lesser known but sometimes very tasty berries are characterized by their long, generally spiny shoots, which usually grow during one season and carry their fruit in the next. They are among the tastiest of all fruits and also some of the easiest to grow. If you especially like currants or gooseberries, then it's possible to fit them into a small garden without too much difficulty.

Raspberries

This deservedly popular cane fruit needs a fair amount of space and is not an ideal crop for a small garden. However, many gardeners will want to try a short row if they like soft fruits, even if almost the whole crop is eaten at one summer party.

Raspberries are at their best when they are grown in a rich, well-cultivated soil that is neither heavy and sticky, nor gravelly and dry; wet, clay soil is especially disliked. Most soils can be improved by digging in some organic matter and raspberries appreciate plenty of moisture, so water well.

Support the plants either on a row of posts with wires strung in between or on trellis. In very small gardens, where there is not room for a row of raspberries but where a few plant canes would be appreciated, two canes can be grown up a single post that can be sited at the end of a vegetable bed or even in a border. This is a rather fiddly way of growing raspberries but useful if space is very tight.

Blackberries

Blackberries are difficult to manage in a small space, as the canes of even the shortest varieties are too long to train vertically and therefore must be tied in along post and wire supports. Blackberries are ideal for training against a fence or trellis, but thornless varieties should be chosen for planting near a path. They enjoy a location with full sun.

Blackcurrants

Good-quality blackcurrants are easy to buy, but if you want to grow your own there are now improved varieties that have made the fruits a far easier crop for the less experienced or busy gardener, superseding most of the old favourites.

Blackcurrants are tolerant plants and should thrive in most soils, while doing better in damp conditions than most other fruits. They appreciate a rich soil that has been improved with plenty of organic matter; they also prefer an open, sunny situation but they do need regular pruning.

Blueberries

Blueberries straight from the bush are delicious with ice cream but they need a very acid soil to grow well (pH4–5.5). So while they can be grown in the open garden in some areas, where the soil is unsuitable (use your pH test kit, page 19) they're excellent in containers filled with an ericaceous compost.

Gooseberries

Dessert gooseberries are delicious and will often produce fruits even when neglected, although careful attention will ensure they crop well. They grow best on a well-drained but rich soil, and in a very small garden are probably best grown as cordons because this ensures that they take up the minimum of space. This system will also make it easier to pick the fruits without getting scratched by the vicious thorns; train them on a fence or on a system of posts and wires. If you have more space, plants grown as bushes will produce a better crop. Be sure to buy plants trained in the style you need.

Red and white currants

It's worth considering growing red and white currants, as again they're not always easy to track down, even on pick-your-own farms. In their cultivation, red and white currants are more akin to gooseberries than to black-currants. Red currants are used mainly in sauces and preserves; white currants are sweet enough to eat fresh.

Strawberries

Perhaps the most popular of soft fruits, the strawberry is not the easiest to grow well. However, modern varieties can give a very large crop from a relatively small space if cultivated carefully. Always buy certified virus-free stock, as these are the most productive plants.

Strawberries grow best in an open site sheltered from strong winds. They will grow in most soils, although heavy soils and sandy, free-draining soils need to be improved by digging in plenty of organic matter. They grow well in containers, which is an ideal method for the small garden. Strawberry pots, in plastic or traditional terracotta, have additional holes in the sides to allow more plants to be grown in a small space. Strawberries can also be grown in the growing bags intended for tomatoes, and it's also now common to grow them in bags that can be hung vertically from a fence or trellis.

The small-fruited but tasty alpine or wild strawberries are best in partial shade and can be planted between cordon fruits or in flower borders.

Rhubarb

Is it a fruit or a vegetable? Does it matter? Like so many other fruits, the arrival of virus-free stock has greatly improved productivity. Rhubarb is happy in most soils that are not too wet, but it likes rich conditions, so dig in plenty — and I mean plenty — of well-rotted manure or compost before planting. Choose an open or partially shaded spot for the best crop.

RIGHT: Gooseberries provide good value for a small garden as they will thrive in most conditions and can be trained on a fence to save space.

OPPOSITE: Blueberries make good fruits for very acid soils or can be grown in large pots filled with lime-free soil.

Chapter 8

Plants for Purposes

This chapter provides a guide to the best plants of different types, the most suitable plants for solving particular problems and those plants that will grow best in different sites and situations. Where no specific varieties are mentioned, any will suit; where I suggest particular varieties this may be for their special suitability for small gardens, their inherent quality, their wide availability – or just because I happen to think they're especially attractive; in many cases others will also be suitable. My suggestions are simply a starting point.

The Plants

This is not an encyclopedia so I have included no detailed plant descriptions. This information is now widely available on plant labels, the web, libraries and other free sources and in the plant reference books on the shelf of even the most reluctant gardener. Instead I'm providing extensive suggestions of plants for different purposes and on grouping the plants together to create the best effect, plus advice on buying plants and raising your own.

Key to plant types

B	Bulb
BP	Border perennial
CL	Climber
D	Deciduous
DS	Deciduous shrub
E	Evergreen
ES	Evergreen shrub
H	Hedging shrub
HA	Hardy annual
HHA	Half-hardy annual
HB	Hardy biennial
RP	Rock plant
T	Tree
TP	Tender perennial
WP	Water plant
WS	Wall shrub

All these terms are defined in the glossary on page 236. For the benefit of North American gardeners, USDA Hardiness Zones are given for all plants except vegetables, annuals and biennials, and temporary plantings.

RIGHT: Mixed border with poppies and alliums.
OPPOSITE: Working with your soil type will ensure that plants thrive.

Soil types

Matching the right plants to the right conditions ensures that they grow well and suffer less from disease problems. Whatever your soil type, there are plants that will thrive there, even if you have soil that is of extremely poor quality.

Clay soil

Clay soil can be very fertile but is also heavy, easily compacted and slow draining. Improving the soil with organic matter will enable a wide range of plants to be grown.

- *Amaranthus caudatus* (HA)
- *Chaenomales*, especially 'Nivalis', 'Moerloosei', 'Rowallane' and 'Geisha Girl' (WS) Z5
- *Choisya ternata* (ES) Z8
- *Malus* 'Golden Hornet' (T) Z5
- *Philadelphus* 'Manteau d'Ermine' (DS) Z5

- *Rodgersia pinnata* 'Superba' (BP) Z4
- *Rosa* (DS) Z2–8
- *Tagetes* (HHA)
- *Viburnum tinus* (H/ES) Z7
- *Vinca major* 'Elegantissima' (BP) Z7

Sandy soil

Improving the water-holding capacity of the soil will allow a far wider range of plants to be grown.

- *Asphodeline lutea* (BP) Z6
- *Berberis thunbergii* (DS) Z5
- *Betula pendula* 'Youngii' (T) Z2
- *Borago officinalis* (HA)
- *Eschscholzia californica* (HA)
- *Fagus sylvatica* (H) Z5
- *Gaultheria mucronata* (ES) Z7
- *Geranium sanguineum* (RP) Z4
- *Juniperus sabina* 'Tamariscifolia' (ES) Z4
- *Phlox*, creeping varieties (RP) Z3–4

Wet soil

Raising the soil level using logs or bricks will create drier conditions that will suit more plants.

- *Ajuga reptans* (RP) Z4
- *Astilbe* 'Sprite' (BP) Z4
- *Carpinus betulus* (H) Z5
- *Mimulus* 'Malibu' (HHA)
- *Nemophila menziesii* (HA)
- *Physocarpus opulifolius* 'Dart's Gold' (DS) Z2
- *Primula pulverulenta* (BP) Z6
- *Salix caprea* 'Pendula' (T) Z4
- *Sambucus nigra* (DS) Z6

Chalky soil

Don't grow lime-hating plants like rhododendrons on chalky soil – it's just not worth the effort.

- *Antirrhinum* (HHA)
- *Buxus sempervirens* 'Suffruticosa' (H) Z6
- *Cheiranthus* (HB)

- *Clematis* (CL) Z4–7
- *Daphne* × *burkwoodii* (ES) Z4
- *Dianthus* (RP) Z5
- *Iris*, bearded types (BP) Z3
- *Kolkwitzia amabilis* (DS) Z4
- *Linaria* 'Canon Went' (BP) Z7
- *Magnolia kobus* (T) Z6

Acid soil

More lime-loving plants will grow on acid soil than acid lovers will grow in lime.

- *Begonia semperflorens* (HHA)
- *Cornus kousa* (T) Z5
- *Epimedium davidii* (BP) Z4
- *Erica cinerea* (ES) Z5
- *Erythronium revolutum* (RP) Z6
- *Lupinus luteus* (HA)
- *Magnolia stellata* (DS) Z5
- *Pieris japonica* 'Debutante' (ES) Z6

- *Rhododendron yakushimanum*, hybrids (ES) Z6
- *Tropaeolum speciosum* (CL) Z7

Exceptionally poor soil

Feeding the soil with organic matter and modest applications of fertilizer will greatly improve the soil.

- *Betula pendula* 'Tristis' (T) Z2
- *Cotoneaster* 'Cornubia' (ES) Z6
- *Eucalyptus gunnii* (T) Z8
- *Hesperis matronalis* (HB) Z3
- *Hippophae rhamnoides* (DS) Z3
- *Ligustrum ovalifolium* (H) Z5
- *Phalaris arundinacea* 'Picta' (BP) Z3
- *Ruscus aculeatus* (ES) Z8
- *Tagetes* (HHA)

OPPOSITE: Good plants can be grown on poor soil if it's improved with plenty of organic matter.
RIGHT: *Dianthus* will thrive on chalky soil.
BELOW: Make use of foliage plants like hostas in shady sites.

Special situations

Even the most difficult garden situations can provide homes for lovely plants, whether your problem is a dark, north-facing wall or a particularly cold climate.

Dry shade
This is the most taxing of garden situations but there are still plants that will thrive.
- *Alchemilla mollis* (BP) Z3
- *Berberis wilsoniae* (DS) Z6
- *Euonymus* 'Silver Queen' (ES) Z5
- *Euphorbia amygdaloides* var. *robbiae* (BP) Z7
- *Hedera helix* 'Hibernica' (CL) Z5
- *Iris foetidissima* (BP) Z6
- *Mahonia aquifolium* (ES) Z5
- *Polystichum setiferum* (BP) Z4
- *Symphoricarpus* 'White Hedge' (H) Z5

Damp shade
You should regard damp shade as more of an opportunity than a problem because a wide range of lovely plants will enjoy these conditions.
- *Camellia* × *williamsii* (ES) Z7
- *Fothergilla major* (DS) Z5
- *Hosta* (BP) Z3–5
- *Impatiens*, seasonal varieties (HHA)
- *Mimulus*, seasonal varieties (HHA)
- *Ramonda myconi* (RP) Z5
- *Rhododendron* (ES) Z2–9
- *Sarcococca confusa* (ES) Z8
- *Taxus baccata* (H) Z6
- *Uvularia grandiflora* (BP) Z3

North walls
North walls are cold and sunless but there are still plants that will do well there.
- *Azara microphylla* (WS) Z8

- *Camellia* × *williamsii* (WS) Z7
- *Chaenomeles* 'Rowallane' (WS) Z5
- *Ercilla volubilis* (CL) Z8
- *Hedera helix* 'Glacier' (CL) Z7
- *Hydrangea anomala* subsp. *petiolaris* (CL) Z4
- *Itea ilicifolia* (WS) Z7
- *Osmanthus delavayi* (WS) Z6
- *Pyracantha* 'Mojave' (WS) Z5
- *Rosa* 'Madame Alfred Carrière' (CL) Z5

East walls

Plants on east walls receive the first morning sun on their frozen shoots and flowers – many object to this but some can tolerate it.

- *Chaenomeles* 'Rowallane' (WS) Z5
- *Cotoneaster horizontalis* (WS) Z5
- *Euonymus fortunei* 'Silver Queen' (ES/WS) Z5
- *Forsythia* 'Lynwood' (DS) Z5
- *Hedera helix* 'Goldheart' (CL) Z7

- *Jasminum nudiflorum* (WS) Z5
- *Lathyrus latifolius* 'White Pearl' (CL) Z5
- *Lathyrus odoratus*, sweet pea (HA/CL)
- *Pyracantha* 'Saphyr Red' (WS) Z5
- *Tropaeolum peregrinum* (HA/CL)

Cold gardens

Cold is, of course, relative, depending on where you live, but the following selection of plants should all suit the coldest areas of Britain and down to USDA Zone 5.

- *Achillea millefolium* (BP)
- *Bergenia* 'Bressingham White' (BP)
- *Calendula officinalis* (HA)
- *Clematis viticella*, varieties (CL)
- *Euonymus alatus* (DS)

OPPOSITE: Hostas will thrive in a site in damp shade.
BELOW: *Chaenomeles* will tolerate a cold wall with early morning sun.

- *Hesperis matrionalis* (BP)
- *Jasminum nudiflorum* (WS)
- *Rosa rugosa* (DS)
- *Sorbus aria* (T)
- *Spiraea* 'Pink Ice' (DS)

Raised beds in shade

A raised bed located in a shady spot is a superb situation for growing choice woodland plants and others that flower in spring.

- *Astilbe* 'Sprite' (BP) Z4
- *Epimedium* (BP) Z4
- *Galanthus* (B) Z5–7
- *Hosta* 'Halcyon' (BP) Z4
- *Pieris* 'Little Heath' (ES) Z6
- *Polygonatum* × *hybridum* 'Variegatum' (BP) Z4

OPPOSITE: Hedging used to provide a natural screen and boundary.
BELOW: A sunny site will support a vast range of plants.

- *Primula*, double primroses (RP) Z3
- *Ramonda myconi* (RP) Z5
- *Rhododendron yakushimanum*, hybrids (ES) Z6
- *Trillium grandiflorum* (BP) Z4

Raised beds in sun

Mediterranean plants as well as spring bulbs are well suited to these hot, dry conditions.

- *Crocus chrysanthus* (B) Z5
- *Crocus speciosus* (B) Z5
- *Cytisus* × *kewensis* (DS) Z6
- *Dianthus* 'Pike's Pink' (RP) Z5
- *Helianthemum nummularium* (RP) Z7
- *Lavandula* (ES) Z7–8
- *Persicaria vaccinifolia* (RP) Z7
- *Pulsatilla vulgaris* (RP) Z5
- *Rosmarinus officinalis* 'Prostratus' (ES) Z8
- *Salvia officinalis* (ES) Z6
- *Thymus* 'Silver Posie' (RP) Z5

Hedging

Planting hedges in a small garden is a risky business because they can take up space that would be better used for more attractive plantings. However, with judicious planning and careful plant selection, it's still possible to make a hedge work well in the confines of a small garden. Dwarf hedges are a good choice if you want to use hedges to delineate areas rather than act as more solid boundaries, and you could also choose hedging plants that fulfil more than one function, such as flowering hedges.

Dense hedging plants

These will make a dense evergreen screen that is suitable if you want to create a fairly solid boundary. They can be trimmed to the required height.

- *Buxus sempervirens* (ES) Z6

- *Chamaecyparis lawsoniana* 'Green Hedger' (ES) Z5
- *Taxus baccata* (ES) Z6
- *Thuya occidentalis* 'Smaragd' (ES) Z2
- *Thuya plicata* 'Atrovirens' (ES) Z5

Spiny hedging plants

Do not use these hedging plants where young children may fall into them, but they're useful for deterring intruders.

- *Berberis gagnepanii* (DS) Z6
- *Berberis* × *stenophylla* (ES) Z6
- *Ilex aquifolium* (ES) Z7
- *Pyracantha rogersiana* (ES) Z6
- *Rosa rugosa* (DS) Z2

Flowering hedges

Regular pruning is essential to keep these both densely furnished and flowering well.

- *Berberis* × *stenophylla* (ES) Z6

- *Escallonia* 'Donard Radiance' (ES) Z7
- *Rosa* 'Iceberg' (DS) Z6
- *Rosmarinus* 'Miss Jessopp's Upright' (ES) Z6
- *Viburnum tinus* (ES) Z7

Dwarf hedges

Hedges are not always used for creating solid boundaries or screening areas for privacy. If you wish to use a hedge to edge paths and potagers or to delineate formal beds, these naturally dwarf plants can easily be kept low.

- *Buxus sempervirens* 'Suffruticosa' (ES) Z6
- *Hyssopus officinalis* (ES) Z5
- *Lavandula* 'Folgate', 'Hidcote', 'Loddon Pink' and 'Nana Alba' (ES) Z7
- *Lonicera nitida* (ES) Z7
- *Santolina chamaecyparissus* (ES) Z7
- *Satureja montana* (ES) Z6
- *Teucrium chamaedrys* (ES) Z6

Containers

Containers provide opportunities to change your displays on a regular basis as well as add drama in small spaces. Containers are not only suitable for flowers, however. Fruits, vegetables and herbs can also be grown in them successfully.

Spring tubs

Plant these in autumn to get a display of spring flowers, plus a few flowers in winter, or plant them in full flower in spring.

- *Bellis* 'Habanera', 'Pomponette' and others (HB)
- *Cheiranthus*, wallflower (HB)
- *Muscari* 'Blue Spike' (B)
- *Myosotis* 'Blue Bouquet', forget-me-not (HB)
- *Narcissus* (B)
- *Polyanthus* 'Crescendo' (HB)
- *Primula vulgaris* 'Wanda' and others (HB)

- *Tulipa,* bedding varieties (B)
- *Viola* 'Angel', 'Penny', 'Sorbet' and 'Velour' (HB)
- *Viola* × *wittrockiana* 'Universal' and 'Ultima', pansy (HB)

Summer tubs

Buy and plant summer tubs in bud or in flower in late spring after the last frost in your area has passed. Keep them fed, watered and deadheaded all summer.

- *Argyranthemum* (TP)
- *Begonia* 'Dragon Wing', 'Olympia', 'Stara' and others, fibrous-rooted (HHA)
- *Begonia* 'Non Stop' and others, tuberous-rooted (HHA)
- *Geranium* 'Maverick' and others (HHA)

OPPOSITE, ABOVE: Box creates a neat formal edging.
OPPOSITE, BELOW: This golden Leyland cypress 'Castlewellan' needs trimming as much as the green-leaved type or it will soon get out of hand.
BELOW: Use violas to stock pots, hanging baskets or window boxes.

- *Helichrysum petiolare* (TP)
- *Impatiens* 'Fiesta', 'Mosaic', 'Swirl', 'TuTu' and others (HHA/ TP)
- *Osteospermum* (TP)
- *Nicotiana* 'Avalon' and other dwarf types (HHA)
- *Petunia* 'Designer', 'Duo', 'Pearls' 'Storm' and others (HHA/TP)
- *Salvia farinacea* (HHA)

Permanent tub plants

A surprising number of substantial plants will thrive in large tubs as long as they are fed and watered regularly.

- *Acer palmatum* 'Dissectum Atropurpureum' (DS) Z5
- *Camellia* × *williamsii* (ES) Z7
- *Clematis viticella* (CL) Z4
- *Fatsia japonica* 'Variegata' (ES) Z7
- *Laurus nobilis* (ES) Z7
- *Lavandula* 'Kew Red' (ES) Z7

- *Myrtus communis* (ES) Z9
- *Olea europaea* (ES) Z9
- *Rosa* 'Handel' and some others (CL) Z6
- *Yucca filamentosa* (ES) Z5

Spring window boxes

Be sure the box is raised so that surplus water can drain away in the winter.

- *Bellis*, bedding varieties (HB)
- *Muscari* (B)
- *Myosotis* 'Blue Ball' (HB)
- *Narcissus* 'Tête à Tête' (B)
- *Viola* 'Angel', 'Penny', 'Sorbet' and 'Velour' (HB)

Summer window boxes

Choose as large a box as possible and keep it well watered and fed.

- *Begonia semperflorens*, fibrous-rooted (HHA)
- *Geranium* 'Sensation' and 'Video' (HHA)

- *Impatiens* 'Accent', 'Super Elfin' and 'Mosaic' (HHA)
- *Impatiens* 'Firefly' (TP)
- *Lobelia* 'Regatta' (HHA)
- *Petroselinum crispum* 'Moss Curled', parsley (HHA)
- *Petunia* 'Fantasy' (HHA)
- *Plecostachys serpyllifolia* (TP)

Permanent window-box plants

While few plants will thrive in a window box over the long term, the following have the best chance, as long as you use a rich compost and water and feed the plants regularly. Make sure that the window box is also not too small.

- *Allium schoenoprasum*, chives (BP) Z4
- *Crocus* (B) Z5
- *Hedera helix* 'Glacier' (CL) Z7
- *Heuchera*, Petite series (BP) Z5
- *Sempervivum* (RP) Z4–5
- *Thymus* (ES) Z5

Spring hanging baskets

Hanging baskets can be planted in autumn for an evergreen winter effect or flowering plants set in place in spring.

- *Aubrieta* (RP)
- *Cerastium tomentosum* (RP)
- *Hedera helix* 'Glacier' (CL)
- *Muscari* 'Blue Spike' (B)
- *Viola* 'Splendide', 'Sparkler', Sorbet' and 'Velour' (HB)

Summer hanging baskets

Keeping summer hanging baskets consistently moist and well fed is the big challenge but one well worth meeting.

- *Bacopa* (TP)
- *Begonia* 'Illumination' and 'Show Angels' (HHA)

OPPOSITE: Geraniums are low-maintenance window box plants.
BELOW: Petunias provide long-lasting summer colour for containers.

- *Bidens* (HHA/ TP)
- *Fuchsia*, trailing types (TP)
- *Helichrysum petiolare* 'Goring Silver' and 'Roundabout' (TP)
- *Impatiens* 'Super Elfin', 'Accent' and 'Tempo' (HHA)
- *Lobelia* 'Regatta' (HHA)
- *Pelargonium*, ivy-leaved types (TP)
- *Petunia* 'Conchita', 'Surfina' and 'Tumbelina' (TP)
- *Scaevola* (TP)

Vegetables for containers

These varieties look attractive and will produce a good crop in patio containers.
- Aubergine – 'Mohican'
- Chilli pepper – 'Apache'
- Cucumber – 'Bush Champion'
- Sweet pepper – 'Redskin'
- Tomato – 'Totem', 'Tumbling Tom Red' and 'Tumbling Tom Yellow'

Fruits for containers

Check specialist catalogues carefully for dwarf varieties or those grafted on to rootstock that keeps them small.
- Apple Z5
- Apricot Z4
- Blueberry
- Cherry Z5
- Citrus Z9
- Peach Z4–10
- Strawberry Z3–8

Herbs for containers

Many herbs have ornamental forms that help you create container productive and attractive plantings.
- Basil (HHA)
- Bay (ES) Z7
- Chives (BP) Z4
- Marjoram (BP) Z3
- Mint (BP) Z4

- Parsley (HB)
- Rosemary (ES) Z6
- Sage (ES) Z6
- Thyme (ES) Z5

Tropical-style summer seasonals

Grow greenhouse plants in containers and move them outdoors during the warm summer months.

- *Abutilon*
- *Canna*
- *Dahlia*, tall types
- *Helichrysum periolare* 'Limelight'
- *Ipomoea batatus*
- *Plectranthus*
- *Ricinus communis*

OPPOSITE: Grow your own cucumbers in a container, raised bed or border.
RIGHT: Sweet bell peppers make attractive pot plants.
BELOW: Chives produce pretty flowers as well as tasty leaves.

215

Scented plants

Do not mix scented flowers that come into flower at the same time or the individuality of their fragrances will be lost. Choose the location of the plants carefully. For example, plants with fragrant foliage that release their aroma when touched are ideal alongside a pathway, where you will brush against them as you walk. Similarly, plants that release their fragrance in the evening should be situated near a seating area, window or doorway where you regularly spend time in the evenings.

Fragrant shrubs

Choose shrubs for different seasons and situations so there is always scent in the garden.

- *Buddleia davidii* (DS) Z6
- *Daphne* × *burkwoodii* (ES) Z4
- *Fothergilla major* (DS) Z5
- *Hamamelis* × *imtermedia* (DS) Z4
- *Hamamelis mollis* (DS) Z5
- *Lonicera* × *purpusii* (DS) Z6
- *Osmanthus delavayi* (ES) Z6
- *Philadelphus* 'Manteau d'Hermine' (DS) Z5
- *Rosa*, many but not all (DS) Z2–8
- *Sarcococca confusa* (ES) Z8
- *Syringa pubescens* subsp. *patula* (DS) Z5
- *Viburnum carlesii* 'Aurora' (DS) Z4

Fragrant climbers

Train fragrant climbers to grow around archways, gates and doorways so that their scent greets you as you pass.

- *Clematis cirrhosa* var. *balearica* (E) Z7
- *Jasminum officinale* (D) Z7
- *Lathyrus*, annual sweet pea (HA)
- *Lonicera periclymenum* (D) Z4
- *Trachelospermum jasminoides* (E) Z9
- *Wisteria* (D) Z4–5

Fragrant roses

Roses combine great beauty and scent. Contrary to popular opinion, many modern roses are as fragrant as the old-fashioned sorts.

- 'Canary Bird' (DS) Z5
- 'Compassion' (CL) Z6
- 'Fragrant Cloud' (DS) Z6
- 'Gertrude Jekyll' (DS) Z6
- 'Madame Alfred Carriere' (CL) Z5
- 'Madame Hardy' (DS) Z6
- 'Margaret Merrill' (DS) Z6
- 'Pretty Jessica' (DS) Z6
- 'Royal William' (DS) Z6
- 'Zéphirine Drouhin' (CL) Z5

Fragrant perennials

People differ in their response to flower fragrance so don't worry if some of these seem less than intoxicating.

- *Aquilegia fragrans* (BP) Z3
- *Clematis* × *jouiana* 'Praecox' (BP) Z4
- *Convallaria majalis* (BP) Z3
- *Dianthus* 'Mrs Sinkins' (BP) Z5
- *Hemerocallis lilioasphodelus* (BP) Z6
- *Hosta* 'Honeybells' (BP) Z4
- *Iris* 'Florentina' (BP) Z3
- *Iris unguicularis* (BP) Z7
- *Lilium regale* (BP) Z5
- *Phlox paniculata* (BP) Z4

Fragrant annuals

Allow some of these fragrant annuals to shed their seed and pop up in unexpected places for some scented surprises.

- *Asperula orientalis* (HA)
- *Cheiranthus* 'Bedder', wallflower (HB)

OPPOSITE: Quick-growing sweet peas (*Lathyrus*) provide annual fragrance.
BELOW: Fragrant *Wisteria* can be trained on walls and fences.

- *Heliotropium* 'Marine' (HHA)
- *Hesperis matronalis* (HB)
- *Lathyrus odoratus,* selected varieties (HA)
- *Lobularia maritima* (HA)
- *Lupinus luteus* (HA)
- *Matthiola bicornis* (HA)
- *Nicotiana* 'Perfume' (HHA)
- *Reseda odorata* (HA)

Flowers with evening fragrance

Flowers whose scent is at its most powerful in the evening and at night are invaluable in the workaholic's garden.

- *Brugmansia (Datura)* (TP) Z9
- *Hemerocallis,* some (BP) Z6
- *Hesperis matronalis* (HB) Z3
- *Ipomoea alba* (HHA/CL)
- *Lonicera periclymenum* (CL) Z4
- *Matthiola bicornis* (HA)

- *Mirabilis jalapa* (BP) Z8
- *Nicotiana,* some (HHA)
- *Oenothera missouriensis* (BP) Z4
- *Polianthes tuberosus* (B) Z9
- *Zaluzyianskya capensis* (BP) Z10

Plants with fragrant foliage

Site these plants so that you can rub their foliage while you sit and rest or pass by.

- *Aloysia triphylla* (DS) Z9
- *Foeniculum vulgare* (BP) Z6
- *Lavandula* (ES) Z7–8
- *Melissa officinalis* 'Aurea' (BP) Z4
- *Mentha* × *gracilis* 'Variegata' (BP) Z4
- *Myrtus communis* (ES) Z9
- *Pelargonium* 'Lady Plymouth' (TP) Z9
- *Rosmarinus* 'Miss Jessopp's Upright' (ES) Z6
- *Salvia officinalis* 'Icterina' and 'Purpurascens' (ES) Z6
- *Tanacetum parthenium* (BP) Z4

Foliage plants

Foliage is the mainstay of the year-round garden, and provides attractions throughout the seasons as it changes colour. And it's not just the colour of foliage that's important; the shapes and textures also play a major role in the look of a garden. Don't leave foliage form and colour to chance; choose the best foliage varieties.

Grey foliage plants

Plants with grey foliage look good when combined with pastel-coloured flowers and foliage in purple or bronze tones. Most silver-leaved varieties enjoy plenty of sunshine.

- *Achillea* 'Moonshine' (BP) Z8
- *Anaphalis yedoensis* (BP) Z3
- *Artemisia* 'Powis Castle' (ES) Z8
- *Caryopteris* × *clandonensis* (DS) Z8
- *Convolvulus cneorum* (ES) Z7
- *Hebe* 'Pagei' (RP) Z7
- *Lamium maculatum* 'White Nancy' (BP) Z3
- *Omphalodes linifolia* (HA)
- *Salix exigua* (T) Z4
- *Senecio* 'Silverdust' (HHA) Z6

Plants with gold or yellow leaves

Try the warmth and brilliance of yellow and gold foliage to bring extra life and sparkle to your small garden, especially combined with blue flowers or bronze leaves.

- *Campanula* 'Dickson's Gold' (RP) Z6
- *Choisya ternata* 'Sundance' (ES) Z8
- *Hakenochloa macra* 'Aureavariegata' (BP) Z6
- *Helichrysum petiolare* 'Limelight' (TP) Z9

OPPOSITE: Scented lavenders (*Lavandula*) are ideal for a small space.
BELOW: *Lamium maculatum* provides good ground cover and edging.

- *Ligustrum ovalifolium* 'Aureum' (ES) Z5
- *Melissa officinalis* 'Allgold' (BP) Z4
- *Philadelphus coronarius* 'Aureus' (DS) Z4
- *Physocarpus opulifolius* 'Dart's Gold' (DS) Z2
- *Robinia pseudacacia* 'Frisia' (T) Z4
- *Thuya occidentalis* 'Rheingold' (ES) Z2

Variegated foliage plants

You either love plants with variegated foliage or you hate them – or you love some and hate the rest. Don't plant varieties on my recommendation if you don't like them.

- *Arabis ferdinandii-coburgii* 'Variegata' (RP) Z6
- *Arum italicum* 'Pictum' (BP) Z7
- *Cornus alba* 'Elegantissima' (DS) Z2
- *Eleagnus pungens* 'Maculata' (ES) Z7
- *Euonymus* 'Emerald 'n' Gold' (ES) Z5
- *Fuchsia magellanica* 'Variegata' (DS) Z7
- *Hedera helix* 'Goldheart' (CL) Z7

- *Hosta* 'Frances Williams' (BP) Z4
- *Pulmonaria saccharata* 'Argentea' (BP) Z3
- *Tropaeolum majus* 'Alaska', nasturtium (HA)

Dark- and purple-leaved plants

When used excessively, dark- and purple-leaved plants can be oppressive, especially in a small garden. When used sparingly, however, they add richness, depth and mystery.

- *Acer palmatum* 'Dissectum Atropurpureum' (DS) Z5
- *Astilbe* 'Sprite' (BP) Z4
- *Berberis* 'Helmund Pillar' (DS) Z6
- *Heuchera* 'Chocolate Ruffles' (BP) Z5
- *Malus* 'Royalty' (T) Z5
- *Ophiopogon planiscapus* 'Nigrescens' (BP) Z8
- *Rheum* 'Ace of Hearts' (BP) Z6
- *Rosa glauca* (DS) Z2
- *Salvia officinalis* 'Purpurascens' (ES) Z6
- *Vitis vinifera* 'Purpurea' (CL) Z6

Trees and shrubs for autumn colour

Many foliage plants are at their best in the autumn. All of the following plants have features in addition to their colourful autumn foliage, however, making them excellent plants for small gardens.

- *Acer griseum* (T) Z6
- *Amelanchier lamarckii* (DS) Z5
- *Berberis wilsonae* (DS) Z6
- *Betula pendula* 'Youngii' (T) Z2
- *Cercidiphyllum japonicum* (DS) Z5
- *Cornus kousa* var. *chinensis* (T) Z5
- *Euonymus alatus* (DS) Z3
- *Fothergilla major* (DS) Z5
- *Sorbus vilmorinii* (T) Z5
- *Vitis vinifera* 'Purpurea' (CL) Z6

OPPOSITE: A mixed foliage border of hostas, grasses and blue spruce.
RIGHT: Maples (*Acer*) give a stunning autumn display.
BELOW: *Salvia officinalis* 'Tricolor' has variegated and tinted leaves.

Plants for seasons

Ensuring that your garden is colourful all the year round is one of the challenges of small spaces. You could create separate beds and borders for each season, or combine a couple of seasons together. For example, you could plant spring bulbs with autumn-flowering plants, so that the bulbs will come into bloom after the autumn flowers have died down.

Winter-flowering plants

In some climates, winter consists solely of snow and ice, so these will tend to flower in early spring.

- *Eranthis hyemalis* (B) Z5
- *Erica carnea* 'Springwood White' (RP) Z5
- *Galanthus* (B) Z5–7
- *Hamamelis*, most (DS) Z4–5
- *Helleborus* × *hybridus* (BP) Z5
- *Iris unguicularis* (BP) Z7
- *Lonicera* × *purpusii* 'Winter Beauty' (ES) Z6
- *Mahonia* 'Charity' (ES) Z7
- *Sarcococca confusa* (ES) Z8
- *Saxifraga* × *apiculata* (RP) Z6

Spring bulbs

This is just a selection of the vast range of spring bulbs you'll find in garden centres and catalogues.

- *Anemone blanda* 'White Splendour' (B) Z5
- *Chionodoxa luciliae* (B) Z5
- *Crocus chrysanthus* (B) Z5
- *Crocus tomasinianus* (B) Z5
- *Fritillaria imperialis* (B) Z5
- *Leucojum aestivum* (B) Z6
- *Muscari* 'Blue Spike' (B) Z5
- *Narcissus* 'February Gold' (B) Z5
- *Narcissus* 'Geranium' (B) Z5
- *Tulipa* 'Little Red Riding Hood' (B) Z5

Summer bulbs

These invaluable companions to summer perennials and shrubs are much under-rated.

- *Agapanthus* 'Headbourne Hybrids' (B) Z8
- *Allium christophii* (B) Z5
- *Camassia quamash* (B) Z4
- *Crocosmia* 'Lucifer' (B) Z7
- *Dahlia* (B) Z8
- *Galtonia candicans* (B) Z7
- *Gladiolus mureliae* (B) Z9
- *Gladiolus papilio* (B) Z4
- *Lilium candidum* (B) Z6
- *Lilium regale* (B) Z5

Autumn bulbs

Bringing a hint of spring to the end of the year, many of these are late-flowering relations of spring bulbs.

- *Amaryllis belladonna* (B) Z8
- *Colchicum speciosum* (B) Z6
- *Colchicum* 'Water Lily' (B) Z6
- *Crocus speciosus* (B) Z5
- *Cyclamen hederifolium* (B) Z6
- *Galanthus reginae-olgae* (B) Z6
- *Nerine bowdenii* (B) Z7
- *Tropaeolum tuberosum* 'Ken Aslet' (B) Z8
- *Zephyranthes candida* (B) Z8

Late autumn-flowering plants

The flowers of these plants extend the season and look good with the autumn foliage of trees and shrubs.

- *Anemone* 'Honorine Jobert' (BP) Z5
- *Aster* 'Climax' (BP) Z4
- *Ceratostigma plumbaginoides* (DS) Z7
- *Chrysanthemum* 'Emperor of China' (BP) Z4
- *Clematis* 'Bill McKenzie' (CL) Z6

BELOW: Summer bulbs such as these striking purple alliums provide structure and interest in a summer border.

- *Fuchsia magellanica* 'Variegata' (DS) Z7
- *Liriope spicata* (BP) Z6
- *Mahonia* 'Lionel Fortescue' (ES) Z7
- *Physostegia* 'Vivid' (BP) Z3
- *Schizostylis* 'Jennifer' (BP) Z8

Long-flowering plants

Flowers that bloom for months are especially valuable in a small garden.

- *Argyranthemum* 'Butterfly' (TP) Z9
- *Aster* × *frikartii* 'Monch' (BP) Z6
- *Ceanothus* 'Autumnal Blue' (ES) Z7
- *Choisya ternata* (ES) Z8
- *Erysimum* 'Bowles Mauve' (ES) Z8
- *Fuchsia magellanica* 'Variegata' (DS) Z7
- *Geranium* 'Wargrave' (BP) Z3
- *Rosa* 'Old Blush China' (DS) Z6
- *Rudbeckia* 'Goldsturm' (BP) Z3
- *Solanum jasminoides* 'Album' (CL) Z8

Flower arranging

Many people like to bring the garden into their home with arrangements of cut flowers, and what better way to do this than to grow your own flowers for cutting. However, in a small garden there is rarely room to grow plants specifically for flower arranging. If you do decide you want to do this, however, the following good garden plants are especially suitable for cutting.

Flowers for arranging

These flowers are all good garden plants from which a few flowers can be cut without ruining the display

- *Achillea millefolium* (BP) Z2
- *Alchemilla mollis* (BP) Z3
- *Antirrhinum* 'Madame Butterfly' (HHA)
- *Argyranthemum* (TP) Z9
- *Callistephus* 'Duchess', aster (HHA)
- *Crocosmia* 'Lucifer' (B) Z7
- *Forsythia* 'Lynwood' (DS) Z5
- *Rosa*, single-flowered varieties do not last well (DS) Z5–6
- *Schizostylis* 'Jennifer' (BP) Z8

Foliage plants for arranging

Foliage is an essential element of formal and informal flower arranging – and the garden.

- *Acacia baileyana* (ES) Z9
- *Artemisia* 'Powis Castle' (ES) Z8
- *Carex comans* 'Bronze Form' (BP) Z7
- *Heuchera* 'Can-can' (BP) Z5
- *Hosta* 'Halcyon' (BP) Z4
- *Hosta* 'Thomas Hogg' (BP) Z4

OPPOSITE, ABOVE: *Ceanothus* can be trained against walls.
OPPOSITE, BELOW: *Aster* × *frikartii* 'Monch' will bloom for a long season.
BELOW: *Achillea* make long-lasting cut flowers.

- *Ligustrum ovalifolium* 'Aureum' (ES) Z5
- *Lonicera nitida* 'Baggesons Gold' (ES) Z7
- *Vinca major* 'Elegantissima' (BP) Z7
- *Weigela florida* 'Foliis Purpureis' (DS) Z5

Plants for drying

Drying in a warm dark place, or even in an oven on a very low setting, will ensure that the flowers last well.

- *Achillea millefolium* (BP) Z2
- *Athyrium felix-femina* (BP) Z4
- *Briza maxima* (HA)
- *Eryngium tripartitum* (BP) Z6
- *Helipterum roseum* (HHA)
- *Limonium* 'Forever' (HHA)
- *Nigella* 'Persian Jewels' (HA)
- *Papaver somniferum* (HA)
- *Rosa*, double varieties (DS) Z5–6
- *Xerochrysum bracteatum*, helichrysum (RP)

Water gardens

Even the smallest garden has room for a water feature of some kind, but when planting the feature it is important that you choose varieties carefully because some can be invasive or dominant. Some plants are suited to deep water, although shallow water and marginal plants will probably prove the most useful in a small garden.

Deep water plants

Check catalogues for varieties whose vigour is appropriate to your garden situation.

• *Nymphaea*, dwarf varieties (WP) Z4–7

Shallow water plants

These plants will do well in water that is constantly 5–15cm/2–6in deep.

• *Acorus calamus* 'Variegatus' (WP) Z3

• *Iris laevigata* (WP) Z4
• *Juncus effusus* 'Spiralis' (WP) Z3
• *Nymphoides peltata* (WP) Z8
• *Zantedeschia aethiopica* (WP) Z8

Marginal plants

Marginal plants are particularly useful for very small water features. The following plants will thrive in soil that is constantly wet and will not object to standing in water for short periods.

• *Caltha palustris* 'Plena' (WP) Z3
• *Iris sibirica* (WP) Z3
• *Lobelia cardinalis* (WP) Z2
• *Mimulus* 'Hose in Hose' (WP) Z7
• *Primula pulverulenta* (WP) Z6

OPPOSITE, ABOVE: *Eryngium* make attractive dried flowers.
OPPOSITE, BELOW: Cut and dry *Achillea millefolium*.
BELOW: Use dwarf water lilies (*Nymphaea*) to fill a small pond.

Wildlife gardening

Thoughtful planting in even the smallest garden can create a valuable haven for wildlife – wild flowers, birds, small mammals, fish, amphibians, butterflies, moths and other insects. Some plants provide protection for the wildlife, while others are a source of food. It is worth doing some research into which plants are native to your area, because native species usually encourage more wildlife than introduced varieties.

Berrying shrubs

The fruits and berries of autumn and winter will bring fruit-eating birds to the garden, even if only for a short visit.

- *Cotoneaster* 'Cornubia' (ES) Z6
- *Cotoneaster microphyllus* (ES) Z5
- *Ilex aquifolium* 'Pyramidalis' (ES) Z7
- *Pyracantha* 'Mojave' (ES) Z6
- *Rosa moyesii* (DS) Z5
- *Sambucus nigra* (DS) Z6
- *Skimmia japonica* 'Foremanii' (ES) Z7
- *Sorbus* 'Sheerwater Seedling' (T) Z3
- *Viburnum opulus* 'Compactum' (DS) Z3

Dense shrubs for cover

Once you've attracted some birds with berrying shrubs, don't forget to provide the visitors with protection. Dense, and perhaps thorny, cover will provide birds with shelter, nest sites and protection from cats and other predators.

- *Berberis* × *stenophylla* (ES) Z6
- *Berberis wilsoniae* (DS) Z6
- *Choisya ternata* (ES) Z8
- *Hedera helix* (CL) Z5
- *Ilex aquifolium* 'J. C. van Tol' (ES) Z7
- *Ligustrum ovalifoliam* (H) Z5

- *Pieris japonica* (ES) Z6
- *Pyracantha* 'Saphyr Orange' (ES) Z6
- *Taxus baccata* (H) Z6
- *Thuya plicata* 'Atrovirens' (H) Z5

Bee plants

Bees not only provide a relaxing sound with their steady droning, but their pollination is also essential to the fruiting of many plants.

- *Berberis* × *stenophylla* (ES) Z6
- *Betula pendula* 'Youngii' (T) Z2
- *Brachyglottis* 'Sunshine' (ES) Z8
- *Chaenomeles*, not doubles (WS) Z5
- *Dahlia*, not doubles (TP) Z8
- *Daphne mezereum* (DS) Z5
- *Malus* 'Golden Hornet' (T) Z5
- *Monarda didyma* 'Cambridge Scarlet' (BP) Z4
- *Origanum vulgare* 'Aureum' (BP) Z3
- *Salix alba* (DS) Z2

Butterfly plants

Butterlies feed on nectar-producing plants from spring to autumn; avoid double-flowered varieties, which often produce little or no nectar. Place some in sheltered spots to provide the butterflies with a cool, dry place for hibernation.

- *Aubrieta* (RP) Z7
- *Buddleia davidii* (DS) Z6
- *Caryopteris* × *clandonensis* (DS) Z8
- *Centranthus ruber* (BP) Z4
- *Echinacea* 'White Swan' (BP) Z3
- *Helenium* 'Moerheim Beauty' (BP) Z3
- *Lavandula* 'Hidcote' (ES) Z7
- *Scabiosa* 'Butterfly Blue' (BP) Z3
- *Sedum* 'Autumn Joy' (BP) Z3
- *Solidago* 'Golden Thumb' (RP) Z5

OPPOSITE: A bird bath attracts birds and looks good among perennials.
BELOW: *Choisya* 'Aztec Pearl' provides cover for birds and fragrant flowers.

Food plants

Growing crops in a small garden can be difficult because many people do not want to sacrifice space that they could use for flowers and other attractive plants. However, it would be wrong to assume that fruits and vegetables don't have their own aesthetic appeal.

Fruit trees

Choose fruit trees that are naturally dwarf or that are grafted on to a dwarfing rootstock and do not require different varieties for pollination.
• Apple – 'Goldilocks', 'Greensleeves' and 'Queen Cox' Z5
• Apricot – 'Delight' Z4
• Cherry – 'Compact Stella' and 'Summer Sun' Z5
• Crab apple – 'Golden Hornet' and 'Laura' Z5
• Damson – 'Shropshire Damson' Z6

• Greengage – 'Early Transparent Gage' Z6
• Peach – 'Avalon' Z6
• Plum – 'Czar' and 'Opal' Z6

Soft fruits

Choose soft fruits for their flavour, their compact habit, heavy cropping, disease resistance and lack of thorns.
• Blackberry – 'Helen' and 'Loch Ness' Z5–8
• Blackcurrant – 'Ben Connan' and 'Ben Sarek' Z3
• Blueberry – 'Bluecrop' Z4–9
• Gooseberry – 'Invicta' Z3
• Loganberry – 'L654' Z6
• Raspberry – 'Autumn Bliss', 'Glen Ample', 'Joan J' and 'Sceptre' Z3–8
• Red currant – 'Rovada' and 'Stanza' Z3
• Rhubarb – 'Stockbridge Arrow' Z3
• Strawberry – 'Bolero', 'Marshmello' and 'Pantagruella' Z3–8
• Tayberry – 'Buckingham Thornless' Z6

Fruit to avoid

Some fruits, and some varieties, are simply too large, take up too much space for the return they produce or are too thorny for a small garden, so consider avoiding these.

- Apples – 'Ashmead's Kernel', 'Bramley Seedling', 'Early Victoria'/'Emneth Early', 'Elstar', 'Gala', 'Golden Delicious', 'Granny Smith', 'Idared' and 'Newton Wonder'
- Blackberry – 'Bedford Giant' and 'Himalayan Giant'
- Blackcurrant – 'Baldwin', 'Black Reward', 'Boskoop Giant', 'Laxton Giant', 'Malling Jet', 'Tsema' and 'Wellington XXX'
- Filbert and cobnut
- Gooseberry 'Howards Lancer'
- Medlar
- Pears
- Plums – 'Bullace', 'Cherry Plum', 'Pershore Yellow' and 'Purple Pershore'
- Raspberry – 'Leo', 'Malling Admiral', 'Malling Jewel' and 'Zeva'
- Sweet chestnut
- Walnut

Vegetables

Choose vegetable crops and varieties that are quick to mature, produce a large crop from a small space, are best fresh from the garden and are pest and disease resistant.

- Beetroot – 'Action' and 'Red Ace'
- Broad beans – 'The Sutton'
- Calabrese – 'Trixie'
- Carrots – 'Nairobi', 'Nantuckct', 'Parmcx' and 'Rondo'
- Climbing French beans – 'Cobra', 'Empress' and 'Hunter'
- Courgettes – 'Defender', 'Kojak' and 'Spremo'

BELOW: Crimson-flowered broad beans, elegant cloches and ferny carrots ensure that vegetable plantings look good.

- Cucumbers – 'Burpless Tasty Green' and 'Bush Champion'
- Dwarf (French) beans – 'Delinel', 'Masterpiece Stringless' and 'Safari'
- Lettuce – 'Blush', 'Green Salad Bowl', 'Little Gem', 'Mini-Green', 'Red Salad Bowl' and 'Sherwood'
- Melon 'Bastion'
- Parsnip – 'Arrow', 'Avonresister', 'Gladiator' and 'Lancer'
- Radish – 'French Breakfast' and 'Sparkler'
- Radicchio – 'Cesare' and 'Palla Rossa'
- Spinach – 'Medania', 'Mazurka' and 'Spokane'
- Spring onion/scallion – 'Ishikura', 'White Lisbon' and 'Santa Clause'
- Squash – 'Western Sunrise'
- Tomato – tall: 'Gardener's Delight', 'Piranto', 'Sungold' and 'Tigerella'; bush: 'Red Alert' and 'Tornado'
- Turnip – 'Snowball' and 'Tokyo Cross'

Ornamental vegetables

Some vegetables are attractive enough to grow in the border and have a good flavour.
- Aubergine – 'Bambino' and 'Snowy'
- Brussels sprouts – 'Falstaff'
- Climbing French bean – 'Purple Podded'
- Dwarf runner bean – 'Hestia', 'Pickwick' and 'Relay'
- Swiss chard – 'Bright Lights', 'Charlotte', 'Fordhook Giant', 'Lucullus', 'Pink Passion' and 'Rhubarb Chard'

Vegetables to avoid

Some vegetables take up too much space or occupy the ground for too long to be worthwhile in a small space.
- Asparagus
- Brussels sprouts (except as above)
- Cauliflowers
- Celery
- Maincrop carrots
- Maincrop peas

- Maincrop potatoes
- Marrows
- Parsnips
- Summer cabbage
- Sweet corn

Single-season herbs

These annual herbs are grown from seed every season and die after harvesting.

- Arugula
- Basil
- Chervil
- Coriander
- Dill
- Lemon grass
- Parsley
- Perilla
- Purslane
- Rocket

Long-term herbs

These perennial and shrubby herbs will give you many years of use from the open garden. They also look and smell good, as well as providing delicious culinary ingredients.

- Bay (ES) Z7
- Catmint (BP) Z4–5
- Chives (BP) Z4
- Fennel (BP) Z6
- Garlic chives (BP) Z6
- Marjoram (BP) Z3
- Mint (BP) Z4
- Oregano (BP) Z4
- Rosemary (ES) Z6–9
- Tarragon (BP) Z5
- Thyme (ES) Z5

OPPOSITE: Ruby chard (*Betea*) is highly ornamental.
BELOW: Herbs can be used as edging for vegetable or flower beds.

Special uses

This is simply a list of plants that are useful in a variety of particular garden situations, plus some plants that you should avoid.

Weed-suppressing plants

These attractive plants will bring colour to your garden and help smother weeds at the same time.

- *Bergenia* 'Bressingham White' (BP) Z3
- *Cotoneaster horizontalis* (DS) Z5
- *Geranium* 'Russell Prichard' (BP) Z7
- *Helianthemum* 'Rhodanthe Carneum' (RP) Z7
- *Hosta* 'Frances Williams' (BP) Z4
- *Lamium maculatum* 'White Nancy' (RP) Z3
- *Persicaria vaccinifolia* (RP) Z7
- *Phlox*, creeping types (RP) Z3–4
- *Pulmonaria saccharata* 'Argentea' (RP) Z3
- *Rosa*, Flower Carpet Series (DS) Z5

Plants for covering manholes

Disguise manhole covers by using recessed planting covers, or set spreading plants alongside them.

- *Calluna vulgaris* (ES) Z5
- *Ceanothus thysiflorus* 'Prostratus' (ES) Z7
- *Euonymus fortunei* 'Variegatus' (ES) Z5
- *Rubus* 'Betty Ashurner' (ES) Z6
- *Taxus baccata* 'Repandens' (ES) Z6
- *Viburnum davidii* (ES) Z7
- *Vinca major* (BP) Z7

Quick fillers for new gardens

New gardens need plants that will quickly make an impact. Some are short-lived; others can be removed later to make way for choicer varieties.

- *Achillea millefolium* (BP) Z2
- *Achillea ptarmica* 'The Pearl' (BP) Z3
- *Argyranthemum* 'Butterfly' (TP) Z9
- *Buddleia davidii* (DS) Z6

- *Chrysanthemum* 'Court Jesters' (HA)
- *Lavatera olbia* 'Barnsley' (DS) Z8
- *Lupinus arboreus* (ES) Z7
- *Lupinus* 'Band of Nobles' (BP) Z4
- *Persicaria bistorta* (BP) Z3
- *Phalaris arundinacea* 'Picta' (BP) Z3
- *Sambucas nigra* (DS) Z6

Easy plants to raise from seed

For newcomers to raising plants from seed, these can be grown easily with little or no special equipment.

- *Achillea millefolium* (BP) Z2
- *Centranthus ruber* (BP) Z4
- *Digitalis* 'Foxy' (HB)
- *Erysimum cheiri* (HB)
- *Iberis* 'Flash' (HA)
- *Lilium regale* (B) Z5
- *Lupinus arboreus* (ES) Z7
- *Lupinus* 'Band of Nobles' (BP) Z4

- *Lychnis coronaria* 'Alba' (BP) Z4
- *Tagetes* (HHA)

Plants to avoid in small gardens

These trees, shrubs, perennials and annuals are simply too quick-growing or invasive for small gardens; and please be aware of local advice on species invasive in your area.

- *Acer pseudoplatanus* (T)
- × *Cupressocyparis leylandii* (T/H)
- *Heracleum mantegazzianum* (BP)
- *Impatiens glandulifera* (HA)
- *Juglans* (T)
- *Polygonum baldschuanicum* (CL)
- *Reynoutria japonica* (BP)
- *Salix chrysocoma* (T)

OPPOSITE: *Lupinus arboreus* makes a large plant quickly.
BELOW: *Lycnhis coronaria* 'Alba' has pretty flowers and foliage.

Glossary

Acid (of soil) With a pH level below 7; opposite of limy. Good for rhododendrons and blue hydrangeas.

Alkaline (of soil) Limy, with a pH level above 7. Hydrangeas go pink; rhododendrons die.

Alpine Small plant from the mountains, usually needing sunshine and free-draining soil.

Annual Plant such as alyssum or zinnia that lives for only one season.

Bedding plant Plant raised in pots, packs or trays and planted out for spring or summer flowering before being replaced.

Biennial Plant such as Canterbury bell or many foxgloves that lasts for two seasons, growing during the first and flowering in the second. Some perennial plants – wallflowers, for example – are treated as if they were biennials.

Biennial bearing The tendency of fruit trees, usually apples, to crop well one year but poorly or not at all the following year.

Bolster Heavy steel chisel for splitting bricks, pavers and slabs.

Bolt To produce flowers or seed prematurely, thereby not producing a crop, especially lettuce and spinach.

Cold frame Low brick or timber structure with removable glass roof, used to protect plants in pots from severe weather.

Compost *1:* Special soil mix for raising seeds or potting plants (seed or potting compost). *2:* Well-rotted vegetable matter (garden compost).

Cordon Plant, usually fruit tree, trained as a single unbranched stem.

Corm Bulb-like structure formed from a swollen stem base, as in crocus and gladiolus.

Crown *1:* The part of the plant at or just below soil level from which shoots develop. *2:* The branched growth of a tree.

Cultivar Derived from "cultivated variety", the correct term for named garden forms of plants; in this book, as is more common, I use the (incorrect) term "variety".

Deadhead To remove dead flowers to encourage the production of more blooms.

Dibber Device for making a planting hole for seedlings in potting compost or the garden. Usually wood or plastic.

Dieback Death of shoot tips due to disease, frost or poor growing conditions.

Drainage The seeping away of water through the soil. Good or free-drained soils lose water quickly; badly drained or waterlogged soils stay wet for a long time.

Drawn Stretched, due to lack of light.

Drill Long, shallow depression in the soil in which seeds are sown.

Earthing up Drawing soil up around shoots of plants, especially potatoes, to exclude light.

Espalier Trained tree, usually fruit, with horizontal branches arranged in tiers.

Etiolated Stretched and pale in colour, due to severe lack of light.

F1 hybrid Usually a bedding plant or vegetable created by crossing two specially selected and highly bred parents.

Floribunda Type of rose with many-flowered heads of relatively small flowers. Also known as cluster-flowered.

Forcing Encouraging early flowers or crops by the use of extra heat or protection from severe weather.

Frost heave The pushing of a perennial plant up out of the ground in winter as frost breaks up the surrounding soil.

Ground-cover plants Plants that spread to create an effective weed-suppressing cover.

Half-hardy Used of plants that grow happily outside in summers but will not survive the winter.

Hardening off The acclimatizing of plants raised in a greenhouse to the harsher conditions in the open garden.

Heavy (of soil) With a high clay content; sticky and badly drained.

Herbaceous Having stems and leaves that die down each year, usually in winter, though not necessarily all at once.

Humus The final result of vegetable matter rotting down.

Hybrid tea (HT) Type of rose with relatively few, large, shapely flowers. Also known as large-flowered.

Lateral Stem branching off from a larger one.

Leaching The tendency of plant foods to drain out of the soil dissolved in the soil water.

Leader Main shoot of a tree or shrub.

Leggy Stretched, due to lack of light.

Light (of soil) With a low clay content; easy to work and well-drained.

Marginal *1:* Plants that like to grow in wet conditions, such as at the edges of ponds. *2:* At the edges of leaves.

Mulch Layer of organic matter or gravel spread among plants to prevent weed growth.

Naturalize Allow plants to grow naturally and with the minimum of attention – bulbs in grass, for example.

Neutral (of soil) Neither acid nor alkaline, with a pH of 7.

Offset A young plant that develops at the base of a larger plant.

Perennial Plant with a life span of more than two years.

pH Measure of soil acidity and alkalinity. pH7 is neutral, below 7 is acid, and above 7 is alkaline.

Pinching out The removal of a shoot tip, usually to encourage branching.

Pricking out Transferring seedlings from the seed pot to a pot or seed tray where they will have more space to develop.

Rhizome Creeping underground stem, as seen in many irises and couch grass.

Runner Stem that creeps across the soil growing roots from the leaf joints, as in strawberries.

Self-fertile Producing fruits or seeds without pollination by another plant.

Self-sterile Not producing fruits or seeds unless pollinated by another plant.

Series Group of very similar plants (usually bedding plants) differing in just one or two details, usually flower colour.

Sterile Not able to produce fruit or seeds.

Stolon Shoot that arches over or spreads across the ground and roots at its tip.

Stopping The removal of a shoot tip, usually to encourage branching.

Succulent (of leaves or a plant) Fleshy; adapted to storing water.

Sucker Shoot arising from the roots of a plant, sometimes away from the main stem or crown.

Tender A plant that is susceptible to frost damage.

Truss Closely grouped cluster of flowers or fruits.

Tuber Swollen underground storage organ developed from a root or stem.

Variegated (of leaves) With stripes, spots, speckles, edging or streaks of another colour, usually white, cream or yellow.

Variety See Cultivar.

Weed Any plant in a garden that is considered a nuisance.

Index

Figures in *italics* indicate captions.

Acknowledgements

Author's acknowledgements

The author has his name on the jacket but other indispensable people ensure that the book looks good and reads well. My invaluable agent Vivien Green handled the business end of things with her usual efficiency and good humour. At Cassell Illustrated my editors Camilla Stoddart and then Anna Cheifetz looked after both myself and the book with cheerful professionalism. The index is by Diana LeCore. Finally, my wife judywhite provided the photographs – and so much more.

Photography credits

All photos by judywhite/GardenPhotos.com except for: pp.4–5, 22, 45, 80, 94, 100, 104top, 115bottom, 130, 171, 172, 177, 189, 205below, 208, 213, 222, 224below, 225: Graham Rice/GardenPhotos.com. p.192: photographer unknown.

Garden credits

p.2: 2003 RHS Chelsea Flower Show; design by Kate Frey. p.13: Heronswood Nursery, Bellingham, Washington; design by Dan Hinckley. p.9left: Frelinghuysen Arboretum, Morristown, New Jersey. p.9right, p.14: 2002 RHS Hampton Court Palace Flower Show; design by Jane Mooney. p.15: 2003 RHS Chelsea Flower Show; design by Mark Gregory. p.16: 2002 RHS Chelsea Flower Show; design by Geoffrey Whiten. p.20: 2002 RHS Chelsea Flower Show; design by Sarah Brodie & Faith Dewhurst. p.24: 2003 RHS Chelsea Flower Show; design by Miss Kay Yamada. p.27: 2003 RHS Chelsea Flower Show; design by Barry Mayled. p.29: 1998 RHS Hampton Court Palace Flower Show. p.30: Portland Japanese Garden, Portland, Oregon; design by Professor Takuma Tono. p.32: 2003 RHS Chelsea Flower Show; design by Xa Tollemach & Jon Kellett. p.36, p.50: Wave Hill, New York City; design by Marco Polo Stefano. p.37: 2002 RHS Hampton Court Palace Flower Show; design by Keith Clarke (KC Landscapes) & Peter Furze (Federation of British Aquatic Societies). p.39: Berkshire Botanic Garden,

Stockbridge, Massachusetts. p.40: 2003 RHS Chelsea Flower Show; design by Marston & Langinger Ltd Conservatory, London. pp.44, 138: RHS Garden, Wisley. p.52: 1999 RHS Hampton Court Palace Flower Show. p.53: 2002 RHS Chelsea Flower Show; design by Carole Nottage. p.55: Osborn Cannonball House Garden, Scotch Plains, New Jersey. p.56above: 2001 RHS Chelsea Flower Show; design by Wyevale Garden Center. p.57: 2000 RHS Chelsea Flower Show; design by Geoffrey Whiten. p.61: 2003 RHS Chelsea Flower Show; design by Poz Marton & Deena Kestenbaum. p.65: 2003 RHS Chelsea Flower Show; design by Judith Glover. p.66: 2003 RHS Chelsea Flower Show; design by Geoffrey Whiten. pp.67, 128: 2001 RHS Chelsea Flower Show. Courtyard Garden. p.71: 2001 RHS Hampton Court Palace Flower Show. p.72: 2000 RHS Chelsea Flower Show; design by Patrick McCann. p.81below: Hadspen House, Somerset. pp.148, 204: design by Jan Waldemath, Portland, Oregon. p.108: 1999 Regent's Park Flower Show. p.114: design by Ian Vickers and Richard Holmes. p.128: 2001 RHS Chelsea Flower Show; Courtyard Garden. p.132: 2001 RHS Chelsea Flower Show; design by Andy Sturgeon. pp.135, 185, 213: 2003 RHS Chelsea Flower Show; design by Cheryl Waller (The Herb Society). p.136: 2003 RHS Chelsea Flower Show; design by Juliet McKelvey & Judith Centre. p.143: Vizcaya Gardens, Miami, Florida. p.148: design by Jan Waldemath, Portland, Oregon. p.150: 2001 RHS Hampton Court Palace Flower Show; design by David Lloyd-Morgan. p.153: 2003 RHS Chelsea Flower Show; design by Thames Valley Horticultural Society team. p.154: 2001 RHS Hampton Court Palace Flower Show; design by Peter Sims. pp.155, 228: design by judywhite. p.158: 1998 RHS Chelsea Flower Show; design by Michael Miller at Clifton Landscape & Design. p.161: 2003 RHS Chelsea Flower Show; design by Gaila Adair. p.165: Nancy Bryan Luce Herb Garden, New York Botanical Garden, NYC; design by Penelope Hobhouse. pp.166, 181, 182, 210: 2000 RHS Chelsea Flower Show; design by Ryl Nowell. p186: 2003 RHS Chelsea Flower Show; design by Sir Terence Conran. p.195: The Cloisters, NYC.